YOUNG
PEOPLE
and their
CULTURE

YOUNG PEOPLE
and their
CULTURE
Ross Snyder

Abingdon Press ⑤ Nashville and New York

Standard Book Number: 687-46792-6
Library of Congress Catalog Card Number: 69-12014

Scripture quotations noted RSV are from the Revised Standard
Version of the Bible, copyrighted 1946 and 1952 by the Division of
Christian Education, National Council of Churches, and are used
by permission.

Scripture quotation noted NEB are from the New English Bible, New
Testament. © the Delegates of the Oxford University Press and the
Syndics of the Cambridge University Press, 1961. Reprinted by
permission.

Poetry on page 195 is from *The Complete Poems of D. H. Lawrence,*
Volume I, edited by Vivian de Sola Pinto and F. Warren Roberts;
copyright 1923, 1951 by Frieda Lawrence; reprinted by permission
of The Viking Press, Inc.

SET UP, PRINTED, AND BOUND BY THE
PARTHENON PRESS, AT NASHVILLE,
TENNESSEE, UNITED STATES OF AMERICA

to

*The young people in high school, church, seminary
whose lives touched their teacher*

*The Dirty Half Dozen
my peer group in young adulthood's culture building*

*T. C. Ross
teacher-leader of a community and church. The adult
guarantor of the beginnings of his grandson.*

contents

intent

Always in every civilization there are persons who live out of values they have felt, thought about, originated. So that they have some integrity about life style. They can be encountered. With them, *life* can be made.

Their life develops—it is a river flowing across a continent, rather than a flutter of wavelets pushed up and dropped by the wind.

To help such young people find each other, grow each other and life world, is what *Young People and Their Culture* is about.

It is all too easy for a civilization to slip into becoming institutionalizations of its sicknesses. And to lose grasp on what is healthy human existence.

This book is a panorama of possibilities, a pattern of enterprises whose horizon is the completely personal. It suggests staging areas where a cluster of people-on-the-make would expand into life rather than shrivel into mediocrity and impotence. And clues by which they could shape a society rather than surrender to massage by the gods of masscomm and stultification by fear of peers.

The momentum which carries through this book might be represented by this line of thought—

> "Once men thought they could relax, live off society. But now we know that becoming human means to take initiative in building the culture in which we live."

> "The only vital culture is a developing one. Just as the only vital art is one where people are still painting."

> "We are too afraid of being a truth. Too afraid of creative differences. Of conflict. Too convinced that 'good interpersonal relations' means becoming an interchangeable part, surface, smoothness, phony."

> "Young people could invent places and occasions where they could find people with whom they could make themselves, and a culture. Where they could be expressive of their truth, rather than conditioned. Where communication and encounter would be here and now events. Where they would bring to focus some very few elemental ideas that shape a world. Where they could test their strength against human need and possibility. Where the inner-personal could become potent."

> "A diffuse, yet distinguishable world youth culture is beginning to emerge. In every community its quality and content can be influenced."

What is presented in this book is a multidimensional thrust—a design of existential world for young people within which many activities can be originated.

Section III parallels each of the previous chapters of the book with more specific leads into inventing what young people might do. The material in this section is a series of "stirrings up" rather than a presentation of meetings "to be put on." Its purpose is to aid groups to invent, create, transform a youth culture.

The call to young people today can no longer merely be "come and be educated." Or "come be entertained by programmed sensations and happenings that others have concocted for you." The invitation and opportunity must be—

Create a world culture—and thus culture yourself.

Be "poetry of the present." Break out into *being*.

Move into a life style of celebration.

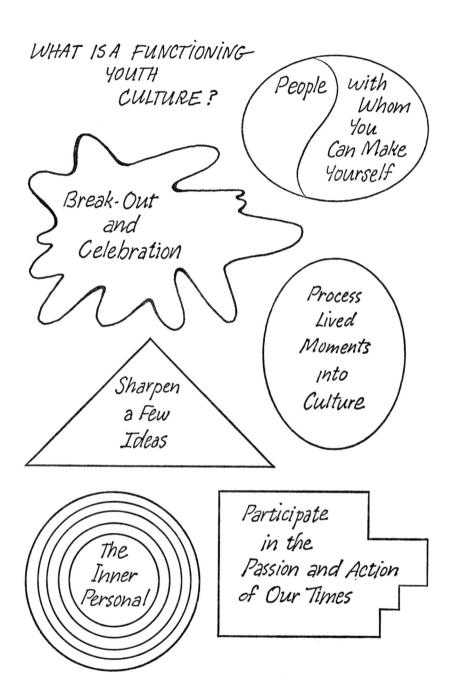

I.

Three Basic Organizers of the Proposal

1. The First Explosion of a New Human Consciousness

We must take seriously the McLuhan hypothesis that the history of man can be broken into three periods on the basis of the predominant style of communication that was forming people.

Communication in Situation

Face-to-face communication formed the mind of primitive man (and the primal originative nucleus of all of us). "Primitive" communication is not only face-to-face, but *in location—in situation where the person is doing things with other people.* They are dancing together, they are fighting a common enemy, they are on the hunt, they are in a family group. The communication is always within a *present field* of forces—composed of the presence of other people and the individual's struggles to get something done. The style is both face-to-face and situational.

Message Via Type

Gutenberg's release of movable type into the educated world imprinted its own quality upon the human consciousness. As the man who reads is prevailingly communicated to, he is looking at marks on a piece of paper, instead of other faces dripping with events and taking attitudes toward him. He is *not in immediate situation*—as, for instance, he was in the days when he would have danced out with his tribe the fight he had just returned from or was just entering. A *reader* can hardly be as organismically stirred, involved, risking, filled with the feel of a supporting group and active memories of other immediate communal experiences as primal man was because of his modes of communication. Getting the message via type does not arouse as much "body" as does dancing and shouting in the dark around a campfire, everybody active, pantingly uniting the tribe back to the ancestors.

In order to receive (or send) a message, Gutenberg man no longer has to be in situation (and if he tried to read while he was in situation, he would be run over!). But he does have available the best that *man even far removed in time and space* has been able to think, imagine, symbolize. Martin Luther or Plato or Confucius can't be here now, but the products of their consciousnesses can—via print.

So *print type communication* gave man a great freedom, great accessibility to products of man's mind. *Meaningful* world suddenly expanded—for everyone that could read. Time and space and particular situation were overcome by the new mode of *shaping the mind communication*. The richly principled, idea-equipped man was now a possibility for many people. A new mode of human consciousness began to take over.

But to the degree that this mode of communication became the prevailing—or sometimes the almost exclusive—mode, man was removed from being formed by immediate situation and the presence of persons perceiving and encountering him. Print communication—by itself—removes man from his fellow man and warm immediacy. A reader can all too easily be rationalized into intellectualistic nonexistence. Thus, print-dominated education leads the person to deal with the surfaces and bones of experiencings, rather than living absorbingly in them. And on into intersubjectivity. Even his own significant feelings become an object to be observed, analyzed, and compared, rather than something which *is* him and *exists* him. By its very *mode* of operation (the media is the message) print communication denied that man was *experiencings*. Man was abstracted.

So it is no accident that some of our brilliant college students commit suicide, because from the very beginnings of their lives they have been alienated from warm contacts with people. Parents and education have told them again and again that reality is found by looking at a piece of paper. Marks on the flat surface of a bit of wood pulp is what wisdom is. For wisdom is to have the right word. Protestantism's basic theology was formed in the Gutenberg era. We have yet to consider adequately what happened to Christianity when Protestants took "word" as the central metaphor for Jesus Christ. Which is one sign that their "classic" theology was formed in the Gutenberg era. Like all other Christians, they were both enabled and trapped by the metaphor-images current in their times.

Electronic Consciousness

Now—McLuhan says—a new human consciousness is being formed by the new pervading mode of communication. The new mode is electronic communication—radio; TV; phonograph records; movies; and, to a lesser degree, pictures taken and transmitted through newspapers. Electronic communication is a new way of processing the world. In a strange way it is bringing back the primitive tribe—in blips through the television set and on the movie screen. The person communicated to is again present in a totalizing situation where everything that's happening is right before him.

He is involved in what is happening in a strange way. He is involved primarily by the sound and his effort to put the blips together into patterns. So—in a new way—man is back now to living in a world of sound and movement.

We do not understand young people unless we understand that music is a primary way in which they create their "world." Many of them carry a transistor radio along with them wherever they go, because for them the world does not exist apart from sound. Without the communication of sound, there is not much communication to the new human consciousness.

Also the new communication is "global"—i.e., a rounded *complex* of sound, sight, touch, lines and shapes, sensations and feelings. The *totalness* of rapidly moving situations is presented. The language of the new communication is not abstract. Primarily, man is a sensing, and he is immersed right in the situation. The situation comes into his room and engulfs him. Such global communication produces a new kind of mind, a new kind of feeling, a new way of being in the world, and therefore a new man.

This new fact of electronic communication is a basic presupposition of our youth work today. For the first time in the history of the world there is a whole generation of this new kind of human consciousness. The prevalent power that is forming this human consciousness is mass communications. Overgenerously available!

This mode of communication is a strange new way of connecting man's body with the world. All he now has to do is to sit in his own room—risking nothing, taking no realistic journey in a world. He is programmed and imprinted by stimuli and sensations selected out for him, so that he will be available in a highly susceptible state to those who must sell him something. Mass-comm is his source of identity, norms, belonging. And in it he lives with a sublime self-confidence.

Enabled by electronic communications, this newness of man lives in the middle of history-making, *simultaneously* with history as it is happening. Ceaselessly news of the whole world is coming at him. And he becomes terribly aware that he's living in history-making. And as a world. What some crazy person does someplace else in a far distant spot may determine our fate and our destiny! There's no longer a possibility of merely personal or merely national history. There's only world history ahead of us and surrounding us. Every young person instinctively knows this.

The death of President Kennedy was participated in by people all over the world. Some of them at far distances participated in it as passionately as we did. So there's no possibility anymore of a little parochial, sectarian approach to teaching about God and God's actions. Now must we develop not only an ecumenical approach to the Christian faith, but a Christian faith that is able to carry on dialogue and communication with people of quite differing interpretations of religion all over the world. We have to live in one world history-making and bring off a world with everybody else. The day of imperialism, when we could cut off ourselves, wall in ourselves and not communicate with other people, is over. Because of electronic communication, it just doesn't exist anymore. The ancient dream that there is only one world is experienced all the time by everybody.

So electronic communications are now enabling some of the dreams of the prophets of old. It's happening. The issue is, do we know that it is, and do we mean to participate in it? Are we going to try to live in a past century, dragging our feet and shouting "no, no" to the new possibility now offered to us?

Electronic communications is also a menace of staggering proportions. It is not clear at all that electronic communications awakens actual participation in the *interpersonal*—a caring about, a co-creating with *persons* in a concrete area of responsible world. Rather it may increase the amount of *impersonal* world, the amount of callousness and violence, the amount of withdrawal into identification with pseudo-persons and phantoms more abstract and contrived than print consciousness ever achieved. It can reduce the individual's world to sound, his mind and psyche to programmed sensations. And those sounds and sensations arise from and through a machine rather than from actual people. The connecting of the person with electronic reality can totally confuse and mislead children, youth, and adults as to what is real. And there are many evidences that this has already happened. The momentum of electronic "possession" tends to lead to atrophy of the central cells of the brain whose function is to hold up immediate emotion, feeling, action, until connections can be made with previous experiences, with the project of this person's one life on earth, with his valuings. Electronic communications can result in the going limp of that function of the human mind which is the self-choosing of directions, the reworking and self-architecting of the inner-personal region. In short, the disintegration of man as *constituting* consciousness, as history-*making*, as living out of principled originality, capable of owning, developing, using ideas. Therefore becoming incapable of a sturdy democracy, of developing the great professions and "minded disciplines" without which a complex society is impossible. All the necessary instruments for the next horrible dictator and the multitude of dehumanizers of humans are at hand. The possibility of living in sensations rather than firsthand meanings, in fantasy instead of encounter, floods the air we hearingly breathe. We have not merely a wasteland, but potential perniciousness of devastating proportions.

We now have before us the first major working hypothesis for building youth culture. The line of insight is—

    a) The prevailing mode of communication is a most fundamental force that forms people.

    b) The new mode of human consciousness is "McLuhan consciousness"—the human existence created by electronic communication. An explosion that is worldwide (wherever the transistor goes!).

    c) With this insight, we will conceive a new kind of education. And a new actualization of a world network of people.

d) We still have the other two modes of communication going on. And *must* have. We do not throw the first two out. Perhaps we must fight to keep them functioning.

Intent

Our task is to combine the three modes into a *system* of communication that will utilize the virtues of all three and try to eliminate the disasters connected with each.

Communication in the context of the lived moment is the ground of thought and society. If a culture is to be more than a shoddy mixture of short threads that pull apart at the least tension, there must be face-to-face encounters and conversation. Experiences here and now must be made sense of by conversation with people immediately accessible. World events have to become interpretations held by those whose lives interweave ours.

And if there are to be *principled* men in our civilization, and men who have command of skills and theory that can bring order out of chaos and professional know-how into the desperate needs of mankind, we must cultivate Gutenberg modes of ordering thought and of communication.

Without this, our civilization would not have available the structuring and infinitely complex and flexible inventing made possible by thoroughly understanding a few focal ideas and the great words of our civilization. Meaning and direction would be irresolute.

To these two modes of "minding" life and of communicating (and therefore cocreating) is now added electronic communications with its global simultaneity, its never-before capacity to present history as it is happening and to dramatically acquaint all people with the infinite depths of the human consciousness.

The vivid use of all three modes of communication and consciousness will distinguish contemporary youth culture from any that might have been possible before.

And only that group of youth who get into masscomm—who do newsworthy things, who create art forms that can communicate their lived moments and express well the present that is bubbling "as of this day"—will make much impression on the culture now forming.

2. The Lived Moment as the Basis of Young People's Growth

The second primary basis of a youth culture is the *lived moment*.

The Poetry of the Present

"Lived moment" is vividly described by D. H. Lawrence in a passage about the *poetry of the present*.

> The strands are all flying, quivering, intermingling into the web. The living plasm vibrates unspeakably. It inhales the future, it exhales the past. It is a quick of both and yet it is neither. The whole tide of all life and all time suddenly heaves and appears before us as an apparition, a revelation. A water lily heaves herself from the flood, looks around, gleams, and is gone. We have seen, we have touched, we

have partaken of the very substance of created change, created mutation. Give me the still, quick, seething incandescence of the incarnate moment, the moment, the quick of all change, the moment, the immediate present, the now. The immediate moment is not a drop of water running downstream, it is the source and the issue, the bubbling up of the stream. Here in this very instant up bubbles. the stream of time out of the wells of futurity, floating on to the oceans of the past.[1]

The nature of youth is future bubbling up through the present. Such also is the nature of Christian existence.

Man lives out of his visioning of future. More accurately, he lives out of a future that is connected with a particular past and is present right here and now. So the proper way to talk about the time with which man lives is not past *and* present *and* future, but future-past-present. One fullness of time all put together. With all three put together, we can live resolutely and in a life world. The past is resource, evidence of ourselves as an identity, background out of which we can emerge. The present—the lived moment—is the reality, but our energies are called forth by the becoming future whose pulse we feel in the present.

The present is where *we* confront the new possibility which God is offering in the situation. The present is the moment for shaping. And the moment when our choice and decision have to be made. We cannot just read about the past and be comfortable because men then said yes to the becoming of their time. We can't live off their "yes" to God. *We* can *live* only in the immediacies of the kingdom of God in each moment of our life. Each lived moment brings a fresh consciousness of time's fullness. And our "yes" will be made because we are able to recognize the presence of the kingdom of God in the situation before us.

And we are alive only in the moment of creation.

[1] *The Complete Poems of D. H. Lawrence,* edited by Vivian de Sola Pinto and F. Warren Roberts (New York: Viking, 1964) p. 182.

28

We Are Meant to Realize Ourselves

"Lived moment" growth fits the emerging new human conscious-ness. It is its essence. Lived moment education is an expression of the contemporary awareness that each of us is meant *to be*— to be *hugely* human.

For far too long, Christianity has come to young people as a religion of "don'ts." "Don't really be anything vigorously yourself. Life consists of not doing what you are commanded not to do. The best way is to stay out of trouble; never do anything much. Particularly on your own. Remain weak and conform. Don't ini-tiate and don't create. And when you are thirty years old, you will suddenly start to be somebody."

But young people of our time are quite convinced that they are meant to *be right now*. And in all the fullness possible for them at their period of development. "Go where you're going to go, and be what you're going to be" is one of the slogans of their time. "Be where the action is" is another. They are no longer satisfied to put their talents in a napkin and bury them in the ground, as the parable of the talents suggests an overcautious adult once did. Young people are out to develop their talents, be something here and now, cause things to happen.

We are moving, then, from a ministry *to* young people to a ministry *of* young people. Young people can cause things to happen. They were meant to be significant, even now. Life, for them, is to find some place where there is something they can move with. So it is right to say, "Don't sit around *waiting* for somebody to start something. Organize a little world that you can manage; contribute to the culture your world can live with."

A Person Knows to the Degree He Participates

This idea of *"meant to be"* also ties in with contemporary theory of how we know anything. "Gutenberg" thinking suggested that we know by being able to read things on a piece of paper. That we know when we are able to write out an examination, giving back to the teacher pretty much the words that he gave us and we put down in a notebook. Today we have no confidence at all in that as a mode of knowledge. "We know truth only to the degree that we participate in it." This is quite different from memorizing the truth, regurgitating beautiful words and sounds that have been heard. We don't know the truth, so this theory of knowing says, until we participate in it. And we know it *only to the degree that* we participate in it.

Thus we cannot know the love of God until we have participated in the love of God. We do not know the meaning of the cross until we have participated in unmerited suffering for the sake of the kingdom of God.

This theory opens up ways of growing-learning-teaching all the way down the line. We no longer begin with an intellectual understanding of an idea and then go out and try to live it. We begin with the lived moment.

Only in the Midst of the World Is Christ, Christ

Dietrich Bonhoeffer's discovery that "only in the midst of the world is Christ, Christ" is another undergirding of the lived moment of education.

It is very wrong to think of Christ sitting up in heaven someplace—if by that we mean that he is safely removed from this world of ours: the world has been given over to autonomous man, and we won't have to deal with Christ until we die. So much removed that we secretly say to ourselves, "Christ may be *symbolically* presented by the rites of the church, but he is not really present in the world."

Young people must know Christ as a reality they come to terms with now. And this they must do in the dense thickness of contemporary life.

For Christ is a power in this world of ours, at work taking into himself the agony, struggle, disasters, and evil of the world; suffering, feeling it deeply. When we are taken into God's love and creativeness, a transformation takes place and new possibility is born into our lives. This process *is* going on in this world of ours. It is something you are asked to participate in.

It is in the midst of the world that God is acting. It is in the midst of the world that God is taking the evil and the disasters and the warfare and the brutalities, and transforming them by his love and creativeness toward something new and fresh. This is where God is and where Christ is. And therefore we know them only to the degree that we get into the midst of the world. But still we have people who think they can have a special little honeymoon with God and Christ in a closet of their own, never risking themselves out in the world where history and mankind are being made.

"World" doesn't necessarily mean "the world out there beyond the ocean." The world is the nearest thou and that group of people with whom and for whom we can live responsibly. "World" means the place where human struggles and need are found by this particular person. Where this particular person can be "for others."

"Only in the world is Christ, Christ" means that the lived moment is where the reality of growth and conversation with God is possible. Education is what can happen when we get ourselves into situations where Christ's kind of transforming has to come off. It is only as we participate in this transforming, redeeming-from-separation activity that we have any chance of really beginning to know God or to know Christ. To be in touch with him. There's not an up-there and a down-here, but only a God in whom the world exists. And therefore a God in whom the activities of this world are taking place. We must get where action is going on if we expect to meet God, because the only place he will be found is in his creating and redeeming.

Christ Taking Form in a Band of Men

With Christ in the world, we are on our way to another basic of contemporary Christian education which comes freshly from Bonhoeffer. Not only must *we participate* in the truth, but the critical issue is the *"taking form by Christ in a band of men."* This, too, is an important religious possibility for our life.

We can no longer say that Christianity primarily is an individualistic kind of a thing. We have not become Christians unless we are part of a group of people in whom Christ begins to take form. (The term "Holy Spirit" could be used in that sentence, and we'd be saying the same thing.) Until we have been through the experience of being bound together into a group of concerned people, so moved by the love and creativeness of God that we go out into all the world to share the love and creativeness of God, we have not yet experienced the depths of the Christian life. All by ourselves we are not yet fully Christians. We are Christians only as we are part of a team, moved, animated, and equipped by the Holy Spirit.

This, too, has great implications as to our educational procedures.

A Lived Moment Includes Its Meanings

A lived moment is not just frantic activity, a rushing from one situation of programmed sensations to another. Nor is it identical with working ourselves up till we and those around us are "high."

A lived moment is a peak experience. Where we experience, somewhat intensely, "I AM." And creation—rather than mere excitement—is coming off. Something new is coming out of everyday mud, so at the moment I am no longer on my way to becoming a clod or froth.

A lived moment is *lived*. Someone is within it—enduring it, tasting it, being expanded or shriveled, enlivened or deadened by it. *And*—interpreting its meaning. That someone is you.

For *what* happens is not so important as how we interpret it, i.e., what it means. The issue always is, not that nobody waved goodbye, but, "What does it mean? What does it mean to be *me*—

this particular fellow—to whom nobody waved goodbye when I ran?"

A lived moment always involves a *selfed* body. It is not a happening of startled molecules, but an event in which *a person* is manufacturing meaning. To be filled with undigested "experiences," with lived moments that never had a chance to grow up, is a self-imposed version of the rat race so prevalent in our civilization.

Interpreting a firsthand experience is an important part of living it. We are built to process moment into meaningful moment. A *human* being has to have a meaningful world in which to exist, and meanings to select out and tune his actions. He has to be the *poetry* of the present, not just the present. Spelling out implications of this emphasis on not only having lived moments, but developing meaning out of them, is much of this book.

At a time when masscomm's flood—radio, TV, the movie, the printed page—is replacing *primary* experiences (those we have in face-to-face encounter and in bringing off enterprises *we* plan) with secondary encounters consisting of blips on a picture screen and page, *lived moments* become overwhelmingly important. For otherwise we live deprived lives, with contrived feelings and packaged interpretations we have been sold. The images and symbols which master our behaviors will not bubble up out of our own creative springs, but will be inserted by him who sells and therefore masters us. And we will never know what is real.

Our creative imagination must be stirred by the lived moments of *our* living. Then we will be all one piece, and a work of indigenous art. *Our* lives will be saturated with meaning.

Intent

What might happen if we thought of our life not as carrying out schedules and programs of learning, but as lived moments—to be initiated, explored, thought over, developed into meanings by which we live?

Is it possible to think of a pattern of lived moments which might be the structure of a youth culture in a community—and of the emerging world consciousness?

In the next few chapters, we will develop six areas of such possibility. Which, taken together, are fullness of life and a workable shape of the contemporaneously human. In which young people would be "the poetry of the present."

3. That Corporate Humanness Which Is a Culture

There is a third basic concept out of which comes the design and programming of a center for building a world youth culture. And that is the concept of culture. Human life is a corporate phenomenon. And therefore we have to be about building that corporate humanness which is a culture. *Human* beings live in a culture, not just a "natural" world.

Man Is Man Only in a Culture

Each of us is a *self-in-culture*, not just a self. We live in culture, and *as* culture. We become persons only with the aid of the culture available to us. Most particularly that part of it which we choose to help create.

Too long we have acted as if each young person *all by*

himself could make up his mind, choose a life style, establish a life world. If only we poured into him enough facts and admonitions and kept him frantically busy. Or kept hands off and let him grow as Topsy into a dead future. Actually he can make up his mind, establish a style of life and life world only *as he is a member of a culture.* Especially one-on-the-make.

Lived moments, meanings, *human* existence can happen *only within* (1) a structure of relationships and joint enterprises, which is also (2) a world of communal language, ground rules for the game of life, expectations of one another to which a number of people give workable assent. These two—put together —are what a culture is.

And that culture has to be built by people; it is not something handed down from the clouds, nor coming to us as our biological heritage, nor is its form dictated by our hungers and instinct. It is a structure of relationships and meanings—a meaningful world—in which and out of which we live together. And it takes working at. We must all get in on the act of building and rebuilding the culture which makes possible lived moments for our kind of fellow man.

Unless we do, we are parasites and nobodies. Never really *knowing from the inside* the truth and the feel of our culture, since we have not participated in its becoming.

Further, to the degree we are non-makers we are allowing a few determined and highly vocal people to tell the rest of us what kind of world we will be permitted to live in. *They* shape our vital space, determine the kind of experiences we will have and the style of life possible for us.

And today—in contrast to stolid primitive societies—we have to keep building and transforming every culture of which we are a part. The only vital culture is a developing one, just as the only vital art is one where people are still painting pictures.

Once men thought they could relax, live off society-as-other people-make-it. But now we know that we must take initiative in building the culture which exists us.

Further, "man come of age" has a desire to build something and not just write his name in sand. When he is healthy, he is a momentum to establish something within which people can relate, have their voice heard, grow. He wants to set in motion a societal institution, whatever it is called, that will continue to influence life. And so be a history-maker of some dimensions.

Therefore, in contrast to organizations working with youth for the sake of *one particular purpose*—such as to make them skilled to earn and consume, or teach them a heritage of sanctions and preferred modes of life, or provide them release and recreation, or make available a programmed sensation whenever they want to turn on TV or a happening—what the young people of a community need are opportunities and places where they can develop a culture, build an indigenous civilization right among themselves and in their town. And have connections across the world.

If we accept "building a culture" as our basic understanding of our operation, then we know what we are trying to do. We will not be meandering around on this or that interesting thing somebody else has done someplace, but we will have an enterprise. And one of dimensions equal to those of youth. It will be an enterprise in building *habitat for human beings*—who are youthful, who are in need of other persons with whom they can make themselves. Our purpose is not just to bring off a mutual admiration in-group (although there will be many such) but to provide meaning-full social ground for young people's lives, and help them learn how to build civilizations.

Not Limited to One Spot or Organization

There is no particular place or institution that must be assigned this possibility of being a center of world youth culture-building. It may mean a new approach to running a high school, teaching a class, being a church—or a community movement yet to be invented, such as a summer youth enterprise. Or a new way of being president of a student body. Or an institute run by young adults in a city.

It may mean establishing an ecumenical youth movement in a community where high-powered young people of various religious faiths can create together something not yet seen in this world—a youth culture established through the working together of many religious heritages and convictions rather than the usual dividing of the capable youth of the community into ineffective insulated cells shaped by adult inability to live in the new age. It will have to be encompassing enough and distinctively intense enough that it can influence community youth culture, yet in small enough units that it is workable and can provide the intimacy and immediacy which youth feeds on. Just another mass machine production won't do. And—as necessary as such places are—it will have to be more than a place of entertainment and recreation. It will have to be a *full* culture, enabling young people to see and put life all together in personal form.

Under whatever auspices and however the program is initiated and constructed, it would see itself as a creative unit of the diffuse youth culture that is everyplace. It would be a place where those whose time has come would live and develop. We are after establishing a functioning culture, a *new* humanity.

But Should Youth Try to Build Culture? Should Not Young People Just Enjoy Life and Go to School?

Youth is the time to begin doing what a person does whose life style is creating culture rather than consuming and conforming to the culture other people apart from him make.

Already there are enough people in the world who are trying to escape into the enclosed sanctuary of an affluent Garden of Eden. Already too many are trying to boat through life in a permanently adolescent Noah's Ark where all is moratorium. Where all they do is to look out at a world in deluge, float in a flood of sensations and perceptions but never land at some particular spot and make it a habitat fit for human beings. We do not need to condemn more people to float up into their adult years with this style of life.

Further, culture-building needs young people. A fresh surge and intensity of feeling is requisite for creation in any field. And fresh surge and wealth of feeling is what youth is when it is true to its own nature.

And young people may not be so embedded as adults are in what already is, and so may be better able to see new possibility. They are looking for an opening in psychosocial space which is theirs, and which *they* can architect and fill. And so may be more sensitive to what is not yet established, but even now is a future present in the present. And being naïve, they try out fresh approaches. This could be particularly true of new fields in which young people have lived all their lives, but to which adults must emigrate.

But youth's advantage is not total nor guaranteed. Primitive legends unite in making the point that the *first* effort by the youthful maker-of-the-new to bring life to his people may not come off. He has to go through struggle, testing, mistakes, before he has the power to awaken sleeping beauty and stir the kingdom from lethargy. So youth, too, is finite and human just like the rest of us. He, too, has to be grown as culture-builder.

In this era of man, how young people participate in forming the culture of their community, of their nation, of the emerging world, is just beginning to be found out. But many youth early become better educated than present adults, become highly skilled in many human enterprises. Their potential pushes them to create somewhere and somehow. Further the whole world is in such a formative, breaking-out condition that we need to rally all the people we possibly can to create a culture world fit for human beings. And this must be done in each community.

We won't and can't bring off this crucial "worlding" without the fresh energy, the capacity to feel, to perform feats of imagination, and to associate with people beyond usual walls—that are sort of givens with young people.

They Are Already Building a Culture

Further, young people are already doing things to each other, already establishing life styles that are acceptable in the peer group; already—wittingly or not—they have a youth culture going. The youth peer culture in every community is already doing things to young life, and too many young people keep silent and irresolute, acquiesce or only gripe about the few focal leaders of the present youth power structure. And so are silent partners in the murder of a good school, in alienated life, in withdrawal into "let them run things."

Today we have new realization of the effect of the youth peer culture upon a young person. We are beginning to have evidence that:

(1) the increase in psychological ill health in teen-agers is galloping.

(2) while childhood and parents are in every adolescent's life story, in and of themselves they are no longer considered adequate cause for the difficulties and sufferings of many teen-agers. An "absurd" teen-age culture is a major factor.

(3) some of the present youth generation are often very cruel, very rejecting, very filled with violence and resentment, very convinced that they should have the world as they individually want it to be and on their terms. When admitted to mental health clinics, they are classified as "character disorders," "infantile personalities."

Jules Henry, an American anthropologist studying youth culture in a large American high school, came to the conclusion that the peer culture of "Rome High School" was "culture against man."

40

There Must Be Able Young People as Pacesetters and Leaders

We have a fresh realization that youth can no longer—nor should they—be led solely by adults. Some youth today are powerfully equipped with ideas and culture. They can set a pace of full living, establish a reference group that guarantees their identity by its identity. No longer are adults and great hero figures the only persons in whom a young person can see and feel "there is powerfully desirable existence," and so through identification with such a person have some sureness about the forward thrust of his own identity. Now each young person looks to see this in other young people.

So today, youth themselves must be "the significant other" who incarnates for other young people desirable existence. Youth themselves must acquire competencies in the logistics of enterprises and relationships. Youth themselves must become the major therapists of other young people.

Not that adults are unnecessary.

Directly working with youth—in creative fidelity to their growth—an adult can function as guarantor, coach, enabling teacher, minister of depth.

Also, what young people today—and this proposed culture enterprise—require are adults who are a liaison with and ambassador from some frontier group of adults engaged in a similar culturing enterprise.

And to get some new things going in the youth culture, a few determined adults need to meet with a few high-potential young people long enough and again and again to establish the beginnings of a communal culture that could contribute to the emerging world youth culture.

Youth Culture Is Youth's Responsibility

Young people's most immediate and responsible creation is forming a youth culture. To meet the needs of their own age

41

group and implement its participation in what's happening. This means that they move the adult community culture at significant points where the new must break out.

A youth culture cannot be cut off from the total culture of a community or nation or world ferment, but it can have some fundamental autonomy. It is that aspect of the total culture which tensely forms youth and their friends. And in which they can learn how to create.

To greater degree than ever before in mankind's experiment, there is a youth culture all over the world. Also in every community. This youth culture (a subculture of the national and new consciousness of man) gives every young person an enveloping world within which he creates many of his moments of aliveness and himself. To some degree this culture is apart from and in opposition to the universe of culture offered by the adult institutions of his own nation. But upon closer inspection may often be seen as a more intense expression of that adult world (e.g., a violent individualism that need not take others' opinions or wills into account).

A present guess would be that world youth culture is propagated and sustained by masscomm, packaged by an adult generation that wants to sell things to young people, and features entertainment celebrities that sooner or later go commercial and phony.

Also within present world youth culture is a world surge toward freedom. And toward a wealth of feeling and meaning expressed musically, in poetry, in TV and movie, in total body action. If McLuhan is correct that a new human consciousness is emerging all over the world because of the very nature of electronic communication, and if historians are correct that now there can no longer be national histories but only world history, then rightfully ambitious young people have a great arena in which to create culture. Whatever they have will be an offering in a world ecumene.

42

What Is a Full Culture?

The task of this book is to architect a picture of a full-orbed culture, that any person's life better include if he wants to be on his way to becoming a human being.

The next chapters lay out six areas of being human. Six areas of lived moments and "poetry of the present" for young people, together with supporting nuclear ideas which could enable us to continually create activities which especially shape man's consciousness and the culture in which he lives.

Here is no program to imitate, but rather patterned possibilities out of which each group must do its own imagination and construction, get themselves enterprises and task forces, grow a culture which sustains young people—and thus grow themselves.

What these are is indicated by the chapter headings of the next six chapters and the development in each. To make "re-memorable" this picture of the lived moments and functionings which must be going on in an adequate youth culture, I have put it all together in one visual design which is at the front of this book. Here is the range of being human that any functioning youth culture should offer. All these activities have to go on if there is to be a *culture*.

Put all together in one verbal picture, this is what is being proposed:

> There are to be places and occasions where young people can find persons with whom they can make themselves, and culture a culture. Where communication and encounter are here-and-now events in the lives of real people.
>
> Where they can break out in celebration.
>
> Where they can be expressions of their truth, more spontaneous than conditioned.
>
> Where they can bring to focus some very few elemental ideas that shape a world.

Where they can test their strength against human need and potentiality.

Where it is possible for each person to grow a rich and resolute inwardness which enables him to be self-propelling with a self-governance system. And to be creative potential, rather than an inwardness of sawdust.

In regard to the need for such, a youth minister writes: "I sense a tremendous need among youth for what you have called 'habitat'—room and a place to live expansively, expressively. This seems to be critical. There is no place for them to 'break out.' To celebrate. As a result of this lack, there is a sense of grayness, emptiness, meaninglessness, confusion, despair. And eventually they find themselves in the prison of hostility-resentment-rebellion. Or else they give up and go dead. There is a deep hunger for life-giving experiences. But a subtle sense of 'It won't ever happen to *me*—I won't find it. I've got to conform or die.'"

II.

Design of a Youth Culture's
Desirable Functionings

4. People with Whom You Can Make Yourself

Young people will run a mile to get away from a place that is cold, where people wear poker faces, where everybody is afraid to let himself come out.

A church, a class, a world ecumene enterprise, a youth center via mass communications—all must be experienced by them as a habitat of the interpersonal. A place where the poetry of the present is filled with warmth.

People are available. They are not cold, indifferent, formal, playing roles, alienated, canyoned on all sides. There is intimacy, flexible enough that a young person can turn off or turn on his participation in it. Little worlds can be formed. The interpersonal is functioning easily.

What establishes a youth crossroads is warmth, intimacy, the actualities of a band of people in whom Christ is taking form.

A team. A youth center and the "immediacies of the interpersonal" are synonymous.

An Organism of Persons

At a conference of youth leaders, a group of young people from a church put on their coffeehouse play. It had finally been written by the director, but it had come from them and they put it on for us, partly creating as they went along. They began working on the play by coming together and talking about the kinds of phonograph records they liked to listen to—which ones said something to them and why. They talked about the television shows that said something to them. They talked about the kinds of experiences they were having in high school that they felt pretty strongly about. They remembered a couple of musical comedies that they had seen—or listened to via records. After they had said all this to one another and to the director, she then wrote the script.

Then they realized that this kind of show can't be produced on a stage way off in front of people, because they'd be denying everything that this play was about. The people must be in an intimate coffeehouse atmosphere, and the "players" scattered around in the coffeehouse itself. The play had to become each time a drama of everybody present, not something that a few people had worked real hard to produce and the rest applauded at the end. The division between spectators and players had to be overcome, but not artificially. The *lived moment* of warmth, intimacy, the interpersonal—into which you can enter if you want to—had to be enabled.

But putting the play on in such a mode did not yet complete the intersubjectivity they were working for. It was important to talk together afterwards. The "audience" talked with the cast and with one another to check out together how they all experienced it and what it meant to them, so that what was in the play could

48

become significant symbol uniting them into one body of humanity.

The cast reported that although this was the fifth time they had given the play—or maybe *because* it was the fifth time—when near the end of the play a girl who had been silent in the back of the coffeehouse suddenly cried out her loneliness, all in the play were hurt once more by this cry, and they tried to reach out to her and get her to come in and join the group. "We go through that experience every time we do the play. It isn't just that she's somebody out there; she also is speaking the loneliness that each of us often feels. And when this poet sitting on top of the stepladder reads Ferlinghetti, we too feel that way, we are waiting for a rebirth of wonder in our schools and in America. And when the girl looks in the looking glass and dreams the dreams she does, we feel that dreaming about the future is not foreign to any of us. And here is Gino, who is quite sure that the only thing in this world is to be brutal and rough and impervious to everybody. That's us too. Each time these characters cry out and talk and say something we take them very personally. And they are voicing *us* as well as themselves. We produce this play as a team, hoping that it will awaken some new life in the people that are present here."

We can now understand what is meant by "a team." It's a group of people who have shared together, been unafraid to honestly state what they feel and think and what their problems are, have discovered a way of expressing all this very artistically in a setting that freshly grabs hold of them and other people. And they have worked together for a period of time. They begin to be a living system that is tuned in to one another. When one hurts, everybody hurts; when one escapes his bondage, all escape bondage. Everyone is participating in the effort to try to heal particular people and the times in which our lives are placed. So that finally others beyond the original group can think and pulse with them.

The heart of such reality is Martin Buber's "I-Thou." As

49

many people understand this phrase, it tends to speak of only two people and also leaves out the necessity of enduring each other and working together over a period of time. But I-Thou doesn't necessarily refer to only two people. It can consist of five or six people, or eight or ten people, who have going one living system that envelops them all, yet makes each one a *particular* one to everybody.

First-century Christians thought of themselves as "a living temple, a habitation for God through the Spirit," "a body that upbuilds itself in love" because each part is moving and performing its function in the whole body. Bonhoeffer's idea that Christ takes shape in a band of men is a striking contemporary image. Chardin has given us the image of the thrust of evolution of our earth as the emergence of a world net of thoughtful men who care about each other and are in honest communication with each other, each hungry to be more than he now is, sensitive to the potentials of NEW TIME. Personal life and Christian life are incomplete—and one has only entered into the outer chambers of complete life—until his life is joined into a living system, an organism-on-the-make, a peopled body.

Remember this group of young people constructing and putting on their play of present immediacy as a picture of the interpersonal which a true group is.

What Goings-on Bring off the Interpersonal?

Leaders of any enterprise need to have a rather full understanding of the basics which bring off their enterprise.

This is particularly true of youth work, since the stakes are so high that false leaders and stupid leaders ought to be ruled out. And it does little good just to keep saying that young people need lived moments of the interpersonal. Leaders must understand *what* the interpersonal is and what processes and kinds of events bring it off. For then they can initiate and improve it as it happens. And the young people of that culture can be enabled to participate in it other than blindly and by happenstance.

What are some workable specifics of what forms the interpersonal?

Meaningful World Is Created
out of and by
All of Us

As many grains of wheat, scattered over the plains, are gathered together in the bread of life for particular people on a particular occasion, so is the interpersonal. The interpersonal is Eucharistic.

Out of the offering from where each is deeply living, meaningful world is put together.

This bit of meaningful world, for the duration of this lived moment, is habitat for each and all together. It is home-base territory, filled with their struggles, tuned with their existence, marked out with the roads of their enterprises. Upon it is their signature. It is territory they are exploring and colonizing together. Which they defend against all invasions and destroyers. Within it all can live and move and have their being toward life rather than toward death.

They begin to trust that the others will be there when needed, to feel that they can count on one another. That the others will not intentionally profane this meaningful world, will not violate anyone's revelation-offering of himself.

The interpersonal is, first of all, a result of cocreation. In the very act of cocreation, something of each brings alive the others, and a field of power comes into being. They are "membered" together into one body. Just to be at home with one another, people have to feel that they are in the same meaningful world. But in the interpersonal, that meaningful world is being *created* by all and out of all.

When such a life style is "the establishment," people can

51

make a very desirable self out of their relationships with other people.

The Interpersonal Is Inter-Consciousness

Each person in this world is a *consciousness*. An awareness that sees and feels the "world out there" and is constantly organizing meaningful worlds in which it acts. An awareness that is capable of understanding, and using symbols.

Only this kind of life can live *in* the world and *with* people, rather than among things. Participate in life *from the inside,* enter into and understand other life. All other modes of life merely *use* the rest of the world in their own desperate struggle to be. And so are condemned to the cold darkness of a thingified world.

But only each particular person "knows" his consciousness (and that not very well!). Each person is *in* his own experiences, his meanings, his body, in a way no other person can be. Each person is a world premiere of *his* particular life story. Each is in charge of his one life on earth—and concerned about it—in a way no other person is. But if he is to succeed, other persons must become knowledgeable about his life story, concerned and involved with his life project. Communication of these seeings, feelings, intendings (that only this particular person is in *direct* touch with) is an absolute necessity. And consciousnesses that communicate with each other have a vastly expanded and enlivened world. So much so that a *human* being is a conversation. An interpersonal world.

The interpersonal vividly uses all that a man's own quite personal consciousness is, but does not remain shut up and solitary to itself. Through communication and cocreation, a person transcends the limitations of just one consciousness, leaps up into a new level of existence. Whereas the *things* of this world are forever self-imprisoned. Being human and being inter-consciousness are inseparable.

The interpersonal then is *inter-consciousness*. A generous giving and receiving. The richness of interiority in each person gets something of itself expressed and is taken understandingly into other consciousnesses. All so involved then exist in *meaningful* world, not alienated world—in personal world, not computer world.

To be interesting (and to be profitably interpersonal), we must have gone places and had considerable feelings and ideas aroused, have interiorized interesting people until their aliveness sings in us, have at least one thing we do fairly well, one interest we really know something about, have mulled over our experiences and let our imagination create.

Without such richness, a person does not have materials with which to build inter-consciousness. Nor can he understand very well another's subjectivity.

So he misses much of the delight of inter-subject transactions —experiencing himself as warmly alive, able to discover, symbolize, communicate, cocreate. Knowing that he is really *in*, not an outsider. That he is the kind of person that some other human being regards as worthy of trust and hope.

One of the intense joys of life is such moments when the wealth of another person's consciousness is being revealed to us, and ours is being received by them. This power of human consciousness to interweave with others' minds and feelings is something to be celebrated, enjoyed, actualized.

For the world changes when we hear the sound of a human voice dialoguing with us, tuned with respect for some experience we are telling about, and what we make of it. When the sound of a human voice and a pair of eyes warmed with interest in us comes through to us. When someone is talking with whom we can just kick things around, test out what we really feel and think without being judged and held all the rest of our lives for what we say.

Unless this reality of discourse is in a youth center, no one will come out in the open, no one will offer. Group creation would be impossible. Since in the interhuman we become different people than we are when we are connected up with an "it" of some sort, all youth work must begin with the interhuman.

Inter-subject

But having celebrated the weaving together of the mind and feelings of many people, we must also point the danger. Each person's own experience and thinking can get blurred into a general mass: the vivid colors of particular ideas get blurred into an indiscriminate gray or one eccentric color which demands that all conform—or else. In youth culture, we must keep in mind also that each person is a *subject*—a unique center of struggle, experiencing, interpreting.

So we have to say that the interpersonal is not only inter-consciousness, but subject-subject. That is, two centers of freedom, each a continuing source of data on life. Neither of us is to disappear. *Inter-subject* does not mean that we are *merged into* the other person. We do not lose our own center of decision and our own content of consciousness. By the very nature of existence, we cannot be the other person. We cannot lose our subject nature—even if we try.

Inter-subject is treating each other as subject-subject—not subject-object, user-used, creator-conformer, judge-culprit, holy man-sinner, responsible-irresponsible. The truly interpersonal is not just "spilling the beans" to each other, a sort of shameless unclothing of ourselves to any and sundry, but is a respect of each other as a rich interiority that is a chooser and decider, a private and unique valuing which we do not invade but invite to offer what it feels to be relevant. We see the other as another center of common humanity. With which we transact.

To establish subject-subject requires not only communication, but encounter. Encountering the other, not in a spirit of trying to destroy him, but of invitation (sometimes even insistence) that he *appear* to us.

Encounter is coming at each other in such a way as to bring each other out from nothingness, swamp, sentimentality. And be not a changing cloud with each puff of wind and supersaturation of climate, but a "thisness" with distinctive style, shape, center, boundaries. We do each other no service when we allow the other to think he is getting away with playing with us, putting us on, trying to misrepresent himself to us. We are no help to another when we excuse irresponsibility, act as if the other were still an infant and a fairly weak person who cannot stand encounter to the degree of risking appearing before us as he is.

Encounter and Conversing Communication

So we have to acquire the life style of encounter and conversation. We have to encounter in situations which awaken and stir up the wealth that is in each of us so that each of us is vividly mind and awareness.

Among other things, this means communication. One revealing freedom talking with another revealing freedom. One freedom entering into what the other is feeling, thinking, intending, standing *with* him in his existence situation until we achieve significant symbol. Communicating until both understand some particular thing that the other feels and intends. And both know that this is so because finally the words and gestures which are used call out in each similar responses.

Really extraordinary conversation is going on. It is not *prattle*—a disturbing of the air with meaningless noises—but *conversing communication*. Meaning by "conversing communication" a running of *"the personal"-which-is-in-the-one* into the other, and a running back of a new person, new meaning, new idea—the original having mated with some "personal" in the other. Conversing communication is communing and cumulating communication. Talking because each wants to be understood by the other and to understand the other. Unafraid to reveal the *actual*—the good and bad, the ambiguous mixture he is of despair and enthusiasm, spontaneity and fear, good and bad judgment.

When we do not reveal the actual in us, we are trying to play a game with the other person. We are not openly saying to him what we really think of him and see him as (but probably feeling it all the more intensely because we now are also sitting on top of our impulse to tell him what he really is—as we experience him). The whole relationship becomes phony, sickening, and all those involved become the very opposite of persons you can make yourself with. Being "kind" and socially smooth is often the very opposite of helpful to the other's growth. And to one's own growth. Finally nobody knows what his truth is, loses all central identity, becomes a cloud of unbecoming. Diffuses into mass man.

Here is a description by a college student of the kind of person he was hungry to meet—

> We are the "impatient generation," unable and unwilling to wait. Our perceptions always have behind them a thrust, a sense of immediate impetus which motivates us to act. Our perspective is not mellowed by time or experience or wisdom. We know only the moment and we respond to it while we can.
>
> We are least influenced by calculation and reflection and careful plodding. The man—the people, with enthusiasm demand our attention and draw us in. Whether it be the enraged draft dodger on the steps of our City Hall or the lamenting Negro mother on her small Mississippi farm, our emotions, our thought, our whole beings are engaged, and *we are forced to come to grips with that reality before us.* Our perception is based not so much on what we have already known and experienced, but more particularly on the demanding passion of that which lies in our immediate present.
>
> He who will "bring us off," then, will be he who is able to arouse us with his own charismatic passion about matters and persons who have personal meaning for us.

We are too afraid of being a truth. Too afraid of creative differences of conflict. Too convinced that good interpersonal relations means becoming an interchangeable part—surface smooth, phoney. And that we must become so in order to get along in the world. A condition all too true of many social worlds that now are—marriages, families, businesses, community institutions, run-of-the-mill friendships, the whole entertainment and leisure-time world.

Could not young people find a way and place where they could be about building a culture that is not so duplicitous, so leveled off to statistical mediocrity, so choking of personally achieved truth and meanings, so much a conspiracy to encourage mutual sickness and infantilism?

Conversing and encounter do not always mean coming directly at each other. They often happen best when together we "bounce off" something we have together encountered and experienced. For then more of us might be awakened than by what we could verbally bring up in a mere conversation. Involved together in an enterprise difficult to bring off, which encounters opposition and significant peak situations, meeting a beauty not our own that overwhelms us—are normal ways and good ways of encountering.

A discussion of a good play or movie we've both attended may reveal more of us than a direct attempt to understand each other. Yet even that is not so authentically revealing as fighting a hard battle alongside each other.

But just fighting the battle or having the experience and talking about one's attitude toward what happened is not enough. We really have not encountered each other until we both try to *art* the experience—that is, to turn it into a significant pattern of beauty and meaning, and *then* discourse with each other. This we rarely try to do. It is not in our present habit patterns or expectancies.

The other day, my wife and I went walking over a mountain slope filled with continual discoveries of new-to-us flowers. From

time to time we encountered an intensely exciting flower inscape
—a patterned beauty that was a 100 percent realization of its
nature. And the whole experience was situated in a horizon of
tumultuous mountains on all sides of the valley. It was a lived
moment that was delight, and we were exhilarating freedom.

But that was not all. That evening we took time to write brief
poems out of the instresses of the afternoon. And then we read
them to each other and talked about each. And much more of
each of us came out—and was received by the other—than in the
first moment of firsthand experiencing. Without this second
phase of reflecting and "arting" our experience, much of us would
have been left unrevealed, and the lived moment would have
remained but a *fragment* of "this is a good happening."

Intimacy

Now we can conceptualize what intimacy and immediacy
are. What processes constitute the real article.

Intimacy is all that we have already talked about—in a
peculiarly intense and inner-personal form. So that it is experienced as a new mode of human existence. It runs all the way from
one person sharing with another his daydreams of future, to a
corporate group whose folkway is mutual ministries to each other.
Where finally one living system of corporate life is achieved.

Unless the universe comes to us—and remains with us—in
the form of particular persons, it is indeed a monstrous, mech-
anized thing. And we are alien. We cannot be an island unto
ourselves. Our completion is "a near Thou"—a particular person
(or body of persons) with whom we can create and be created
over a period of time. *Together* we are a human being. Inter-
connected. Hyphened, so that feeling and fate and fortune flow
back and forth and envelop the whole. We are *tuned in* to each
other. One living system, with two centers, warmly enveloped.

And we are tuned in to not just the fringes of each
other's personality—the instrumental "using-and-manipulating-

the-world-for-our-own-purposes" habits of our life. The tuning in-to, the interconnectedness, the hyphening is of the *inner-personal* region of each of us. Where *we* live. *We*—not just our ideas, our chatter, our achievements (or lack of them), the words we have learned from our culture—are communicated. In intimacy, we feel that we and the other are using *speaking words*—words that express what deeply we are and are formed by. For intimacy comes from an expressive life, rather than a reactive or defensive life. And whenever we sense the other as threatened, reacting, defending, intimacy disappears.

Neither can intimacy be forced. It is an *expressive spontaneity*. It is not routine, but must always be freshly emergent.

However, intimacy inevitably involves some duration through passing moments. A person can hardly feel treasured if he has suspicion that tomorrow morning or next week he will be despised, laughed at, the moment of intimacy violated and profaned. So creative fidelity is a built-in component of intimacy—until some pernicious alienated culture pressures us into believing otherwise. The very impulse of intimacy is not enjoyment of one's momentary sensation, but a feeling that this relationship is good and the beginning of creative fidelity to the growth of this new level of being human.

Intimacy is a dwelling of the other in one's consciousness. We can all testify that in peak moments of achievement, disaster, choice and intense feeling, we carry on a dialogue with some "significant other" in our own internal speech. Not to be given the answer, but as part of the process of arriving at an answer.

Youth can grow up within the church who have competencies to create social worlds whose quality is intimacy, whose structure is inter-subject. Tough-fibered young people who can fight battles and not yield their integrity. With sustained power to encounter—to get at what is real and vivid in one another, to bring one another out of nothingness and sentimentality into existence.

To a world so desperately in need of it, they will be *sources* of transforming love.

Intimacy with the Pulsing of Some Culture

Depth and enduringness of the interpersonal is dependent on more than just the presence of other people. It also requires intimacy with some pulse of culture-building. An intimacy that unites us with *a people,* with more than just two or three others, with more than disconnected moments. Ultimately, in making ourselves, we transact with some culture. Not merely with individuals or even an intimate group, but with "my people."

Intimacy with a culture and *a people* means to sense the originative nucleus of the heritage, to dialogue with it, to encounter its integrity with one's own integrity. It means also to reconstruct the expression of that pulse, revitalize and purify the tune and the beat. For that is the only way there can be a living tradition.

The young person or adult who has lost intimacy with some forming tradition is lost. He is left with only his own hungers and a statistical judgment of what the large number of people are now doing. He has nothing to awaken his imagination except his own concupiscence. Nothing to culture his consciousness or nurture his intense feelings on into meanings. Nothing but his own anguished howls and the fashion and hit of the week.

And he has no ample identity. For much of any person's identity comes from knowing and believing the distinctiveness and rightness of the culture which has produced him and in which his life is situated. Not that it is perfect, but that it is worth throwing one's life into its future. A person's most rooted identity is his sense of "my people."

Too easily we can give up the deepest meanings of America, of democracy, of the Christian church, and join three groups of people—those who are rootless and have disinherited themselves, those who would like to see such traditions terrorized and destroyed, those who pretend that their own greatest apostasies and profanations are identical with the originative realities of America, of democracy, of the Christian pulse.

But the racist, the raw individualist, the libertarian, are not expressions of the pulse of life of either America or the Christian church—much as they continue to be very vocal and often determine what we actually do. To a considerable degree a civilization is what goes on in it—not the phrases we use in talking about it. But the American experiment and the Christ enterprise are also the deeper promises which are always working away, to which each generation can give its energies in a fresh way. Knowing that there will never be a perfect world—except in the chatter of naïve propagandists.

Many things that we all resent in our civilization are the defects that are part of a technological, commercial, mass-entertainment, affluent war society. These dehumanizations we have to fight against. And we can fight in the name of humane values and sensitivities that are, with us, traditional—i.e., we believe them to be of more than passing significance, not just accidental. Rather they are fundamentals of the personal.

But how many people are willing to make such a fight is always a question.

Let us have intimacy—I-Thou—with some basic heritage. But not unthinking and uncreative conformity—to either tradition or what presently is.

And if we are to escape the walls of being just nationalistic or provincial or barrenly "getting ahead in the world," the dialogue will have to be with a religious heritage. One that is on-the-make, able to handle a technological society and world history-making, one which overcomes rather than buttresses walls between men and layers of elect superiority. And no religious tradition is presently perfect on these requirements. Which is another reason why we must dialogue.

5. Break-out and Celebration

Celebration and "break-out" is a second kind of activity that has to go on at any place we're expecting young people to be and to grow.

Young people were not meant to be always cautious, unalive people. Part of the secret of life is every so often breaking out of the limits that have been imposed on us and that we have imposed on ourselves. To some degree every teenager must break out of the limits of his own home and his own church, his own community *and his own peer group.* He must not be entirely dominated by them. Because if he is, he will grow up being just another conforming non-entity. He won't be of much use in this world because he will be unindividuated mass man—ruled by anonymous "they."

All of us, in order to become individuals, do have to break out. Most teachers and parents try to keep youth from breaking out. And that is one necessary function, because if a person broke out all over the place he'd become psychotic and alienated. Each teen-ager has to work through a continuing struggle. On one hand there has to be an *ordering* of life if there is to be either character or community. But also he must free himself from the things that have been preventing him from making his own decisions, exploring the wide, wide world, and organizing freshly desirable world!

Risk

Therefore, today the word "risk" is a crucial one for Christians and for young people.

First of all, because many young people misunderstand what is meant be risk. Risk isn't a senseless trying to prove that you're not afraid to play Russian roulette—holding a gun barrel against your head (or somebody else's head) and pulling the trigger on the chance that the gun isn't loaded in that chamber. Nor is risk taking LSD. Risk is not roaring down the road on a motorcycle, weaving in and out of traffic.

Risk is calculated. Risking because something needs to be done, and you're "it." Risking for some growth and development. Breaking out of a treasured sin and fear you've had all your life, feeling that you no longer have to accept its limitation. Most of us repress our good impulses and are strong on remaining hidden and feeble in risk. Risk says, "Look, break out of this cautious limitation of your goodness. Break away from your habit of never speaking out. Sortie out of where you have been concealing yourself."

Risk is speaking up and getting out before other people what you really feel and think. It is breaking through the customary ways of family, school, church, society—not just for the sake of rebelling, but because you cannot in good conscience any longer participate in some stupidity and injustice. You must give voice and action to protest and discontent—which, if not divine, is at least human.

The major break-out now in our America is that of the black man. How he does it, and how the white man relates to all forms of the break-out, is much of the drama of our country's future. The white too, must break out and risk.

Risk, truly understood, is a major impetus and habit of religious life. A fundamental of Christian existence. Without this element of risk, there is no cross bearing toward rising with new life.

Really, we were not meant to be humdrum. We were meant to be an aliveness. Meant to insert our lives where the action is going on, get into a main river of activity, rather than staying in a muddy back eddy, swirling in its littleness. From time to time we must sail out of our accustomed habitat; not that we disdain it, but in order to get the experiences of being where other things are going on that can wake in us depths we do not even yet suspect. We are built for risk—not just to have kicks, but "for the sake of" and "in the name of."

Release from Tensions: Becoming Once More One

Another mode of break-out is release from tensions, from the rat race, from governance by the clock.

Have you not experienced that the pressures upon you are such that by the time Friday night comes, you've about had it? The tensions under which everybody is living and relating today are such that release of some sort is indispensable. But of what kind? Unless we can provide good ways of doing this then obviously we all find not-so-good ways of doing it. For certain people, getting dead drunk over the weekend is one way of releasing tension. A vast number of laborers do this, and a vast number of top executives in the suburbs do this. Some wives in the suburbs drink because their lives are so cabined, confined. Some people go to LSD to expand consciousness, al-

64

though probably it's finally a fragmentation and constriction rather than an expansion of consciousness. And a constriction of human relationships.

The Watusi (or whatever becomes the latest dance) is one communal form of breaking loose into a oneness of vitality. That it always is, is doubtful—just watch the faces.

Insofar as any mass release is made a substitute for a healing breakout *in the situations that cause the tensions,* the participants are condemning themselves to a breaking-out of symptoms all their lives. For they are evading handling what causes the tensions. Some forms of break-out are a mode of fatalism and resignation to the status quo. They are opiate of the people.

Perhaps the most used way of freshening ourselves is just sitting around, talking about what has happened or should happen.

Or breaking the momotony of our own stream of consciousness by putting on a hifi record we want to hear. Or turning on the radio and TV and going off in an imagination we didn't create. Letting the imagination go as it is massaged by masscomm into a fantasied world of the absolute freedom and superman existence which exists only in the electronic entertainment world, is probably the most used of all methods of breaking-out of what is. This method is particularly tempting to an adolescent who feels that no one understands him (or her), that he is the victim of no-good parents and a no-good world.

Just for the Fun of It

Dance; singing; playing in a jazz combo which creates as it goes along, each sensitively responsive to what the other is doing and letting the melody line take all kinds of shapes; athletics; swimming; surfing—all the modes of total absorption and whole-bodied functioning—are breaking-outs. Losing one's usual self in the out-of-doors or in a new social situation, opening up a new interest and expression of self-to-be-developed, are other kinds of pushing out into new staging areas of aliveness. Go ahead and imagine in your situation all kinds of ways of letting go tension and functioning just for the fun of it. Ways that create fellowship and freshness and aliveness in persons. The crucial thing is to be committed to this way of life.

The three essentials seem to be a spirit of playfulness, imagination on the loose, and a congenial group.

It's great to be spontaneity bubbling in immediacy. Freely being itself—unexpected, unprogrammed, "poetry" of the creative present.

Great is imagination which takes into itself the experienced realities of life, sees in them possibilities, constitutes a new life world for us. Great is inventive imagination which is eternally the "producer" that begins every break-out from what is. Through the whole course of evolution, it has been the main agent.

A youth center is a perpetual invitation to inventive imagination. And a place where many can learn dependable ways of breaking out.

Communal Celebration

Celebration is the warriors of a tribe dancing out around the tribal fire the battle of that day. Retasting its crises, exultations, frenzies, suspense. Re-citing particular deeds of individual courage and extraordinary skill. Reliving the whole struggle with increasing intensity each time round. Once more expressing in moving form the innermost movings of their history. Calling to witness, offering their warfare to, binding their group back into The People who were at the origination of things. Into Our People moving through time with destiny and distinctiveness.

Celebration is Moses climbing up to the top of Mt. Pisgah, and there at the peak recalling the escape from Egypt and the wanderings and trials even as he sees into the Promised Land— which he will never reach, but his people are journeying toward. And being content to have shared in his people's saga, even though denied forever the achievement of the goals of his life and the completion of his people's journey.

Celebration is entering into the passion of a life lived with absolute intensity toward the coming of the kingdom—in faith that even most desperate struggle and the darkest defeat would be transformed into New Time. Experiencing the august solemnity of love.

Celebration is the tuning of persons to each other and to caring and to destiny, until there breaks out in their midst the Holy Spirit. And out of them rush speaking words that can be understood round the world wherever persons are.

So deep rooted is celebration in the innermost moving of life that communal celebration is part of all true corporateness.

What forms might it take? What may be contemporary expressive contents and significant acts of communal celebration?

Contents and Mode

Contemporary celebration will still be celebration of the innermost moving of all life—and not of our arrogance and idolatries. Celebration must be an escape from the latter. Tempting as it is, in communal celebration we are not trying to say, "Look how wonderful we are. Nothing like us ever was. Whatever we are and do is what LIFE is."

Celebration must use the idioms and art forms of the emerging new human consciousness—this new era of mankind which is a new style of communication. Such new idiom, style of communication, mode of consciousness, pacing and punctuating is a startling requirement.

Musically, contemporary celebration will have to select out and use rhythms and tunings of young people's present ways of symbolizing deep movings. It must always reject the phoney, the commercial, and that which misshapes life. And therefore, among other qualities, it ought to be not "smooth," but vital, rich in actuality, saying well and exactly the consciousness it is

67

trying to express, never stereotyping everything into a dull sameness.

Practically, this means the use of a jazz combo that is not compulsively wedded to one style of jazz, has a wide range of feeling expression, has played together long enough that the players sensitively get the feel of each other as persons creating, and each is competent and free enough to improvise. For if there is to be (as there must be) *poetry of the present,* the jazz combo is one place it must be happening. Singing groups and guitar soloists also fit. The sound of a guitar seems particularly to resonate with a simple, direct, personal "testimony": "This is the situation, and I am the person who is in it. This is how it seems to me and this is how I feel." Said preferably in original lyrics, or in singing well-chosen contemporary songs.

The mode and quality of the *sound* is the basic of any contemporary celebration. Life world must be built up acoustically in a celebration and interfused with memorable phrase.

Also interfused with moving dramatic image. For mankind's emerging consciousness "thinks" with global feeling images (this has always been true of basic man). Celebration can quickly be killed with too much talk—and too little feeling and imaging of possibility. "Rational" discourse is primarily for another time. Celebration is the time for entering into, appreciating, enjoying, dramatically re-enacting, dancing in all media. Though some explosion and focus of an idea should occur at some insightful point.

"Moving dramatic image" is all kinds of contemporary art forms—particularly original creations by the celebrating group. For celebration is the deepest form of poetry of the present. And stale packaging (and by a psychologically distant person) is hardly an experience that right before our own eyes creation is happening. So that we know creation continues, since it is moving among us and within us.

"Moving, developing image" primarily means "hunks of this

group's experiencing still pulsing with life." Celebration is the tribe dancing out *its* battle. And as of that very day. Whenever we get too far from this, we are staging something, not having a celebration. This does not mean that all past is ruled out, but that —as in the tribal dance—present experiencing is the focus and momentum.

And if we are to "dance out" our story of the experiencings we are having, our mind has to grasp *some thread within those experiencings* which makes sense of them—which makes them an exciting plot, a drama of meaningful world. We have to find or create a meaningful story which tells what was really happening in the events—so that we can not only understand *it*, but can understand and handle the next events that come along. "Myth" is the most accurate word for this "story within the story that interprets many stories." It is not easy to invent a myth, though we should always be trying for the one that authentically presents what is freshly present in our experience. Usually we will find ourselves using some version of the great myths of mankind.

The great danger is that we use for our interpretative myth one that we have been sold. One that has been so smoothly insinuated into our unconscious—or into the verbally organized part of our consciousness—that we do not even know that we are using it, or that its truth ought to be questioned. And if it is true that the myths offered the American people for some time through mass culture are "negative, deterrent, even satanic," then every time we construct a celebration and try to interpret some moving event, we can be in a productive battle of choosing the myth by which we celebrate. Our present problem may be that the myths now widely used make celebration impossible. For primarily they wail and deny that sense can be made out of anything. And so we have no "people" that is ours, whose fate is our concern, whose origins contain seed of new life. But are left with the myths of alienated man, lost in exasperated impotence.

69

Pattern and Episodes of Communal Celebration

Every youth center should be exploring this high art form and designing celebrations for their communal group. So that out of many attempts, shape, style, method forming theory will become widely established and available.

What wisdom can we offer on the design-pattern and possible stages of the journey a communal celebration might take? The order is not necessarily the same always, nor are the components. But a *complete* celebration probably involves the following.

First of all, a celebration is of a people, and by a people. A particular group that has been through some common experiences and fate is doing the celebration. You cannot have a celebration by collecting a crowd of spectators and outsiders.

This particular group who have been through common experiencing also see themselves as part of a human enterprise setting out through time toward a destiny. They together can say, "*My people*—in whom I live and move and have my being. Even though I disagree and protest many things about them, their struggle is my major habitat."

Much of every celebration is imaging and arting these two aspects of being a people.

Secondly, every celebration must recount firsthand vivid experience—and process it on into meaning.

Often the experience is but a very simple event of that day—that has hidden in it a fragment of what life is. Or a concern that has welled up since last the group met. Or an event that has in it more than can yet be understood. A celebration properly includes a "liturgy of this day"—which includes not only personal experience, but also lifts up news items of that day which then are interpreted in terms of "the liturgy of profane life" and the "Christ liturgy."

Some dramatic story of "how the future becomes present" organizes every history and every people. Every celebration will have within it as organizer and pivotal constancy the originating myth which makes such sense of life for this people. Along with this story of origination, some moving image of the new possibility in history-making to which their lives can be relevant must be presented.

In all celebration a pervasive style of life is being lifted up all the way through. But it is also good to take some time to highlight it. Preferably with a presentation of vivid experience that had this life style. Accompanying the experience, and interpreting it, should be banners, re-enactment, or other "art of a people."

And—as with all worship—at some central point in a celebration there is offering of self and group and world to transformation.

Intent

Communal celebration is an important and timely mode of breaking-out for young people.

It fits the needs of youth, the style of existence they crave. It fits the emerging human consciousness. It fits the nature of vital Christianity.

If a group of young people could invent a great number of ways of breakout celebration, then they'd be on their way.

Often they will see celebration as a form of worship. As a liturgy that is adequate for this moment of man in a world ecumene. Such celebration will not try to supplant the liturgy of the Sunday morning service—although that too should be open to inventing forms that will be our generation's contribution to the treasury of Christian worship. But in the meantime, let young people create celebrations for the youth culture of their community, and for any task force that has some tremendous experiences.

A youth center is a place of contemporary communal celebration.

71

6. Process Lived Moments into Culture

We all need to rally help to interpret the flood of stimuli which comes at us everyday.

Things are constantly happening—in the world at large and in the places where our more personal "to be or not to be" struggle is situated. Other people's *interpretations* of life, meanings which they recommend, blips and fragments of culture, come at us—through personal encounter, electronic communications, reading. How are we to relate to all these things which are thrown at us?

Many of the things that happen are insignificant and on the fringes of life and our interest. Others come directly at us, and we have to understand their thrust and structures. We must make sense out of what friends, employers, teachers, propagandists, government are doing and hurling at us.

For a *human* being (as contrasted with a "thinged" body) is an understanding potentiality-for-being. If we can't understand fate-filled events and persons, violence is done to our nature as a human being, and we are dogged with basic anxiety. Without understanding, we are torn at and carried toward a mad whirlpool at the bottom of a rapids by forces dark, unknown, impersonal, un-get-at-able. If we misunderstand, we are even more battered and bruised, for we keep doing the wrong things.

Of all in the world, we have ourselves to understand. We exhilarate when we discover there is something important moving inside us. And that we can communicate these discoveries.

For we are clearing up *what* we are. Existence clarification is going on. And to the degree we communicate to others what we find, we are creating the system of meanings by which a group of fellow human beings live.

Create the Meanings by Which You and Yours Live Through Arting What Is Stirring

We are just at the beginning of a vast program of young people producing their own expression of the meanings of their personal experiences, of the history-making happening now, of current TV-movies-records. A center of young life needs indigenous songs, music, poetry, coffeehouse plays, photos, movies, liturgies, nonverbal art.

In my own teaching we use a number of art forms to try to get down to the preconscious and as-yet-unsymbolized wealth of feeling-intending. For the students are so verbally oriented they can roll off papers that don't mean much to them, with very little of their reality in them. Their occupational hazard is changing Christianity into *word* games—as it is for every church member. So in classes in Christian Existence and in Contemporary Religious Experience they are asked to come in each Monday morning with a *nonverbal* symbol of something that has awakened in them through the study and discussion of the last week. Something which *they have freshly created* over the weekend. Which represents a "stirring," not an *idea* they're trying to sell us. So, abandoning verbal symbols, they come with paintings, collages, clay, wire and steel constructions, music, dance.

Then we break into groups of about eight people to nurture it from there on. For the purposes we have, we never criticize the product—either as art or as content—but receive what is and let it awaken us. Nor do we begin by asking the "artist" to explain his work. An individual puts his work out in front of the group, and everybody looks intently at it for some moments in silence—so that the art form gets to them. The looking is being sensitive to what is the organizer (highlight) of the design, what feeling tone the color and form communicate, what pulse of life animates the style and composition. We *first* have a responsibility to discover *what is here*—as we see and feel it.

Then we go on to reporting what it stirs in us. After about fifteen to twenty minutes (sometimes longer) we ask the creator to tell us whatever he wants to of his experiencings while he was arting. How his muscles and arms felt as he worked at it, how breakthroughs came, the drama of his thinking as he was trying to symbolize, and so forth. Then we enter into general conversation with him, building up the meanings we now feel are in it (i.e., what it mates with in our experience, creating something new; how it makes us alive, expands and organizes the world we live in).

It is quite important that the "teacher" also create and that his work go through this receiving and culturing by the group. For an onlooker and invulnerable critic destroys the climate of intersubjectivity and common human finiteness.

What we are proposing is a use of art as part of a process of developing meanings, that is a group enterprise over a period of time. That combines individual solitary germination of one's own stirrings with group culturing and delight in each other as equals.

Such arting is in violent contrast to the increasingly frequent "contemporary art weeks" some churches now hold. This latter is a spectacle. Inquisitive spectators come and pass along "on the other side," muttering such things as "I don't like that," "That I approve of," "Why didn't he paint it this other way?" Such exhibits and treatment are a profanation of the function of art in human experience.

So we're out to develop arting as something done in and by a community. And to find ways where, in an intimate group, we sit down and talk over with each other what we do and the meanings that come out of it. Only then will we be treating art and the artist respectfully.

Why is arting so important in our growing as persons and as a society?

Not primarily as a relief interlude—to rest up from too much verbal pyrotechnics, from too many demands to produce. Arting does something that otherwise may never get done. It enables us to *realize*. Music and the plastic arts most nearly resemble the breaking-out dynamics of the ocean of feeling which man primarily is, and the totalizing purposings and hungers he is when he is all put together.

Art can most accurately and fully symbolize man's *full* consciousness. It puts the contents of his consciousness together in an allness very difficult to achieve in any other way—except through action. Perhaps only arting can faithfully portray flowing process world (the only kind there is) and at the same time set such a world going inside us.

For the primary processes of life are not thought or verbal processes, but intendings and feelings. These basic processes are preconscious—*before* thinking and feeling-intending have become separated from each other. Before conscious and unconscious have parted company.

We *tune into* our fellow man, and we tune into God—through feeling.

Feeling is not the same as a flood of sensation and reaction to what has just happened (i.e., an emotion). Feeling is more primal and more enduring through time. It is the way we sensitively participate in life. Feeling is our *thrust into life*, aware of

75

itself and appreciating itself, tasting itself. Feeling is participating in events with the all of ourselves, valuing their possible outcomes for a *selfed* body. Feeling is more than intellect, but involves it. It is basic *caring for and about* one's self and what happens in the world.

The quality of this primary process is the first important thing about any person.

The quality of your preconscious is your primary relating and redeeming power in any dealing you have with somebody else. Ideas which you have will be received only if, first of all, this other kind of encounter and communication of primary process has taken place.

It is most important for our own growth, therefore, that we invite basic feeling to well up and express itself. That we nurture it, help it mature. For it is source of self-propelled growth for us—and also the propulsion. It has in it the new which we are not yet, and the continuity with what we have already been.

But we do not merely let it express itself; we *art* it. We nurture it on into *significant* form, into *meaningful* world.

We have to art it, because primitive feeling is almost always conflictual, ambiguous, impure, more than one thing, a diffuse field of tensions, often overdetermined by first perceptions. We must art it.

Arting is clarifying, intensifying, imaginatively designing into significant form some emerging stirring within us. And having *consummatory delight* in the process and product.

Not that it is perfect, but that we have gotten it expressed and into form. With all its limitations, it is honestly from our depths and is not altogether bad. Something of us has appeared in time and space and is distinctive aliveness for us. A good thing has happened.

Preliminary to arting is exposure of one's self to vitalities, patterns of beauty, pulsing life, fields of tension—so that something is stirred in us and starts to image. Then comes a time which is often called reflection upon the experience we have had. But more properly is seen as a time of relaxed allowing of diffuse feeling to well up into image and become the burgeoning center of new intense growth in our consciousness. We invite it to do so, rather than command it. For feeling wealth cannot be commanded, and the pulsing new cannot be called by name to come forth. If it could, it would be the old or a fabrication of what we think we *should* feel and see. Like a free adolescent, the new comes and goes as it will! And immediately leaves when criticized.

Given these two initial steps, the arting begins with the vital center of a total complex of experience that begins to grow and organizes the whole field. With the aid of all that we are, it creates a new field of consciousness. This is what imaging, or imagination, is. Imaging and imagination—the most potent agent of creation of future and man's participation in *human* evolution!

Much of arting is the next step—a more consciously directed clarifying, focusing, and intensifying of the wealth of feeling. A moving to put what is still a *weltering* within us into *significant form.*

Then our skills in "architecturing" come into play. The wealth of all that we previously were enables choice of symbols and patterns. A cohering and integrating—not only of this experience, but of it with other experiences we have had—subtly goes on. Shapings are tried—"No, that doesn't express it quite right; this does it better." Organizing meanings and insights pop up—sometimes the right ones, sometimes we keep on groping for others.

For art is not just improvisation, but construction—tenacious work until the product forcefully says what is to be said. Just as poetry is not mere howl, nor a person a mere acting out of impulses. The work—to be *significant form*—must have *style,* distinctively accomplishing what it sets out to do, achieving elemental form rather than cluttered diffuseness. Artistic skill and reworking is required.

And finally—to be *significant symbol*—it must be understood

77

by some communal group. Not identically, for that would be to constrict its wealth and life-enhancing power. But sufficiently in common that it coheres these people into a *common field* of talking, of being with each other, of meanings. And they all know that this is so. Because they have cocreated with each other with its help.

Mind, self, and society have once more been created—by this art product and process.

And also identity. For dependable sense of identity comes from being able to look at some *objective manifestation* of one's self from deep inside, rather than anxiously asking "How do I feel?" and trying to discover self-identity through merely verbal means. With great relief we can present to ourself, "Here, in action, is what appeared. It took on this shape, when I was *freely being.* Not trying to please anybody or conform or sell something, but letting my 'isness' be born. And what came could be understood by my peers. It made sense to them. This is me— at least a hint of where and what my aliveness is. It came up. Now I know something of the submerged furnace of potential that is below what I usually talk."

The question "Who am I?" tends to throw us into anxieties about social status, our niche in the social system. And into highly abstract definitions which we try to manufacture. Whereas the end product of arting reveals *"What* am I?" And with that we can make some progress.

But note that we do verbalize, trying also to find the right words and phrases to symbolize what appears in the art form. We do talk together so that the artist has opened to himself even more than he had recognized. And so we end up not as the *alienated* artist that so often "art" contemporaneously is, but bound together in a sensitive, pulsing corporateness. For such arting and receiving each other's products builds up an intersubjectivity, the like of which the world has very little.

Plus the added confidence that we are beginning to acquire a dependable way of bringing up and culturing the ocean of

78

feeling and preconscious wealth that's inside us after events and encounters.

The Documentary Image

In our work of theologizing and realizing what self-in-world we are, we find very productive another kind of "growing" activity—selecting out and creating the documentary image. "Get that picture of a lived moment in life-as-it-is-going-on, that documents what is life world for you."

Photography, too, is an art form. When it is *making* a picture. Sensing the revealing moment and situation, seeing the significant form in the welter of world before us, getting the lights and darks in juxtaposition so that the aliveness of the field of tensions is communicated, is high art. And if we are to succeed in it, it must become so much a part of us that we can do it instantaneously—right on the spot as we participate in moving life. This arting is not done alone, in the quiet of a room, with the privilege of reworking and remaking, as is true of many other art forms. And always there is the welcome presence of *actuality*—of objective world that has to be dealt with partly on its terms and while it is in motion. Life is that way!

Making pictures (as contrasted with going out and indiscriminately *taking* snapshots) is an excellent way of discovering what's inside us. And of training ourselves in arting as a style of life. We become aware of good habits of perception, of what significant form is, of the vitalities that drive the world right here and now.

And we begin to discover what we want to make a statement about. Simultaneously we learn about ourselves and our world. And how significantly to put them together as self-in-world.

In the class in Christian Existence, each member of the class goes out into Chicago and takes photos of something going on which strikingly presents the life world he and his generation can be relevant to. Trying for that one picture that best documents a crucial emergent in the present human enterprise. Presenting not his own subjective emotions, anxieties, alienations, but an objective human situation-condition in a decisive moment of revealing itself.

Then at a given date, we put up all around the room everyone's choice documentary photo. Sometimes with a brief quotation beside the photo that might increase the "go" of our minds and feelings as we look at both picture and quote. We spend a morning together finding out what they do to us. In long-term deposit, we have in us fresh richness of firsthand material when later we discuss "Who are my people? What ideology for us?"

Recognizing, choosing, *making* a documentary photo is an enterprise involving global sensitivities for seeing, skill in architecting significant form, built-in theologizing. Properly done, it is a deep mode of being-in-the-wrold. And of the new style of theology.

Writing Can Also Be an Arting

Another process and form which we use in realizing the shape of things out there, and of discovering their half-hidden and all too diffuse meanings-for-us, is in writing haiku. Which are but a genotypical example of all forms of writing which follow this art process—poetry, free verse, contemplations, coffeehouse plays such as described in the chapter on the interpersonal.

A haiku is a Japanese poem of three lines. Since the Japanese language, on the whole, consists of short words, under haiku discipline you learn to suggest a lot with just a few sounds. The first line consists of five syllables, the second line is seven syllables, the third line is five again. This forces you to meditate and meditate and meditate on what the essential "gist" is that you want to say. Everything nonessential has to be left out.

A haiku is not a haiku, however, if you write plodding prose. To be sure, a haiku does not have to rhyme, and that frees us to write honestly. But it must be poetry—you have to have a kind of picture in your mind that you're expressing. Some vital moving writes the haiku. A hidden insight that puts things together *freshly*. Often the last line is a bit of a surprise. But the crucial fact is that a haiku is a very fundamental image of some "isness" seen in some very concrete event or part of nature. Hidden in the seventeen syllables is a meaning that the reader may not get until he has read it many times. But after it comes through, he has discovered a meaning that sticks and sticks and says to him. A haiku is a very adult achievement and ought not be attempted by children.

At a conference of adult leaders of youth, they were asked, on the spot, to write a haiku out of an interesting encounter they had recently had with some person. One person wrote—

> Tree softly whispers
> Arms extending, reaching out,
> Brushed by frantic world.

To me, this is a haiku—a memorable image of existence in today's world. Sense the juxtaposition of "brushed by frantic world" and the tree arms softly extending. The writer has caught a particular "thisness" which documents world.

How much of life can be condensed into a haiku! And how much arting, concentrating, distilling, goes into the process. The very limitation of syllables forces this, as well as the inherent concept of haiku. Writing a haiku forces one to take time to contemplate—just what did I see? What is revealed here? And not hurry it, nor accept the first surface grasp. We experience a new self in us—one able to sense depth, that does not have to rush, that is an artist.

After you have done several, take the experience of writing haiku as one memory symbol of the consummatory delight of all turning of experiences into celebration, of all transforming the raw stuff of events into meaningful world, of all changing of lived moments into culture. Without doing such things, you are missing half of your life and desecrating the rest.

Phenomenologizing

We also find it very helpful to acquire the skills of phenomenologizing. Which is a disciplined way of doing what we are doing most of the time in a very fragmentary way—i.e., trying to grasp what *really* happened in an experience, and what it tells us about ourselves and what life is about.

Some experiences seem unusually full of "more than meets the eye." Such lived moments are worth nurturing in such a way that we develop what is *within* them.

The first step is to describe as fully as possible exactly what happened *as it happened.* Don't put any judgments upon the good or bad of what happened or the people involved. Just be a scientist and describe this *particular* lived moment.

But do include what went on "inside" you. For that is a crucial part of your story of what happened. It is being honest enough to make clear that your story is always the lived moment *as you saw it,* as *you* experienced it. Your story is not—and cannot be—an impartial, objective account that everyone would know about. And therefore, you must include what feelings you had as the situation developed, the flow of attitudes and intendings you were acting out. You try for the fullest and most accurate account of the lived moment as it was experienced by you, as it appeared to you within it.

You can do this by writing it out, or by telling it to a "receiving" listener, whose function in the conversation is to help you clarify to yourself what went on—particularly within you.

The second step is this. With this documentation of its immediacies before you, you try to determine, "What *kind* of transaction was going on here? What would I name it? What made this the kind of lived moment it was? What processes were going on?" You are still sticking to what was really within this particular experience. You are trying to comprehend what was here—what its pattern and line of development was. Was it, for instance, really an act of injustice? Was it love—or naïve excitement?

82

From looking at and naming this particular experience, you are forced to work on "What is love, anyway? Just anything anybody calls 'love'? No." As best you can, from this experience and that of other people, you try for a picture of the *processes* which love is—anytime, anyplace. So that you can understand and handle *many* situations, novel situations you have never before been in. So that you will not be sold the spurious article and be played games with.

Working along the lines of this first and second step of phenomenologizing, Gabriel Marcel did a memorable job on "what is involved in being *with*, rather than *alongside* another person?" Kierkegaard worked out what dread is, and the process of becoming an authentic person rather than a phony.

Max Scheler's analysis of the process of resentment is a famous achievement of this second step of phenomenologizing. It enables us to understand many things that happen in this world. And to heal resentment in ourselves and the social scene—if healing is desired (most of the time it isn't).

Step two, then, is an attempt to see the *basic* processes that are at work in the lived moment. To discover what processes *make* certain kinds of life worlds—loneliness, communion, expansion of consciousness, the lived moment of choosing, of celebrating, of arting. Always, phenomenologizing is penetrating into *what is*.

In this second step, we also reflect upon what this experience reveals about us. About our dynamics and the way we are organized. Such as catching—

the particular mixture of good and evil, of defeat and success that I was here;

what I really want out of life—as revealed by what I did here;

the kind of sensitivities I have, as revealed by the way my conscience hurts and thrusts me toward fresh growing;

what I am true to: what is true to me;

what is my truth? When does it come out?

There is yet a third step. What statement can you now make about what a *person* is, what reality makes life possible at all?

You are trying to create a philosophy-science of the becoming which pervades the world.

What does it mean to be a person? From reflection on his experiences in the agonizing destruction of the first half of this century, Martin Buber came to assert that the fundamental structure of human life is I-Thou, and that this nature of man cannot be violated with impunity.

Also, one tries for "What is the nature of the Innermost Moving of the world? What kind of creating and transforming God is credible?"

Man is the most sensitive research instrument we have. Of all the forms of life in the world, he is the most intimately connected with the Innermost Moving. He must *use* his historical lived moments and his own experiencings—the peak ones—to seize such discovery.

Meeting an Integrity

Experiencing an integrity who has had vivid experiences in today's world, *and* has phenomenologized them enough that he has some insight into them, is another important mode of creating the culture out of which we live.

Instead of arguing with us abstractly, such a person sets a model of how to profit by experience, how to make sense out of the events of life. And he enlarges our own area of experience, so we are not confined to just our own—as if it were the only source of truth.

And we probably cannot understand ourselves very well until we've deeply understood somebody else.

This assertion takes us back to the gestalt principle that we can't see anything except as against some kind of contrasting background. We always have to have something *against which* we see. We can see ourselves only in contrast to some other person or some group. Just as we never really "see" depths of our own civilization until we live in and study another culture. (This gives an interesting theory about one use of the Hebraic-Christian epic—what if peoples of all cultures saw more penetratingly into their civilization against the common background of a non-national, non-commercial religious culture?)

But to return to meeting an integrity that has some core of understanding out of which he lives: young people need exposure to adults and young people who have had significant *contemporary* experiencings. (None of this "Now when I was a teen-ager," or "This happened once to somebody I read about"; the only talk permitted is about what risky, fresh encounters and discoveries are happening right now, and what sense we make of them.)

The day is over when adults—parent, teacher, fellow citizen—were meant to be nonentities when around young people. Faceless, feelingless, never having meaningful experiences themselves, just smiling benignly like the Cheshire cat. Such adults are not only useless, they are pernicious. For they telegraph, "Don't ever grow up. The world of adult life is grim dullness and apostasy." Adults also are to be *persons*. To be sure, an intensity of a kind that doesn't overwhelm young people. Young people will know there has been *meeting* when they've encountered such persons—and that adults can be encountered. They begin to feel, "There's a substance and quality here that I don't push around easily and out of shape, but it is friendly to me."

The range of persons young people "meet" need not be confined to those who can be geographically present. There are dramatic ways of presenting the crucial experiences of a contemporary man—and what interpretation of his experiencing enabled him to live them rather than be victimized by them. "Dramatic" is important, for that is the style of consciousness electronic communications is producing in young people. If the material is to awaken and be interiorized, it must be packaged in dramatic form.

85

It is possible to select from a man's account of his experiences a series of excerpts and vignettes that present the simplified fullness of his story. Then interweave these with music which carries the fundamental feeling tone and allows time for the mind to digest each excerpt and be ready to hear the next one. The music can be selected from the vast collection of records now possessed by a group of young people, or it can be original lyric with guitar going on and highlighting. The "show" can be produced live, or recorded on tape and played to the group.

For my own nurture—and that of my students—I have done this with a number of people. For example, from the World War II decade, I have put Frankl's *From Death Camp to Existentialism* in a fifty-minute tape with short musical interludes. At the relevant time in our class enterprise, I invite the class to my home to listen to the record. We agree ahead of time that after we have heard it we will sit in silence for a while. And if some prefer to leave and think about it by themselves, they should feel free to do so. About half do leave, for the story is deeply moving, and it is often more important to let what has been stirred in oneself go on developing itself, rather than murder it by group discussion. We try to keep the talking together from turning into the usual discussion of whether he did the right thing, or how wonderful a man he was, or how dastardly the Nazis were. For we are after existence clarification. We are all instinctively measuring ourselves against what we have heard, even while ostensibly we are intensely trying to symbolize "*What* is here? What has come through to us?" Without making a wooden procedure out of it, we are using the three steps of phenomenological construction.

Bonhoeffer's *Letters and Papers from Prison* can also be memorable. I'm inclined to make this a live production, with one person being Bonhoeffer and seemingly thinking out loud as he writes of an experience, with a man on the guitar singing or merely playing the feeling existence of that moment.

The production of such shows by a small task force of young

people, preferably done in a home or in a *small* coffeehouse round, is one of the productive experiences of any youth center. For we are dealing not with fantasy stories of "trips," nor distortion of life in electronically programmed sensations, nor the wail and sentiment of weak people, but with *actuality*. This is real. It happened as a man tried to make his way in this precarious world. And this is what he made of it. If there is anything we all need today, it is some evidence of what is real. And of the actuality of a *self*-in-world.

Producing such programs is one of the better ways of entering into another person's experience until it gets through to us. So the primary gain is by the few who work on it.

In such activities we are clearing up our own existence, we are arting an imaginative vision of possible humanness for ourselves, we are creating an indigenous culture with which "our group" feels life, makes choices, holds conversation, moves toward its destiny.

Looking Skeptically and Appreciatively at Current Pop Art

If so much of the content and tuning of the consciousness with which people now live comes from masscomm, then we ought not merely be victims of masscomm, but ought to keep analyzing what it is trying to sell us, and how well and truthfully it is arting life. The "McLuhan consciousness"—if civilized man is to survive—ought not just "happen" with a total lack of intellect and critical analysis in a group situation where public opinion can be formed.

Some churches I know show a fairly recent standard movie on the first Friday night of the month. The first purpose is to provide young people and adults with a "vocabulary" of today's human situations (hunks of lived moments) with which to think about life. The movies are chosen with this purpose in mind. The second purpose for such a church program is to build up

87

sensitivities to what makes a good movie, and grow the idea equipment and group methods for establishing what interpretation and style of life is present in any dramatic entertainment show—movie or TV. For if people today are primarily learning their tastes and hungers, their ways of feeling and choosing, from dramatic electronic presentations, then they must acquire competencies in analyzing what is being said—else they will lose charge of their own lives to the conditioners and massagers hired by masscomm.

So after the showing of the movie, a panel of three persons starts off the analysis. As in phenomenologizing, the first effort must be to establish just exactly what was here—

Where was the most vivid scene for you? Why?

Which character did you most identify with? How describe his life style?

Overall, what's the way of being-in-the world that this movie presents? The story of life it recommends?

Then, having done that, they come to such questions as—

Is this story honest, or is the movie maker playing games with us?

Is this mode of being-in-the world a live option, or something to be avoided like the plague?

After about fifteen minutes of the panel, everybody gets into the act, and later refreshments are served.

Public opinion about how to live *their* lives is built up in young people by the TV shows which every young person must be able to talk about, else he is not "in." To analyze such shows —particularly music platters—is a very risky business. For it is very threatening. Young people have so identified with the shows they are accustomed to turn on, and they live so much in an acoustic world of sound and beat, that almost any analysis threatens their own identity. It is perceived as condemnation of themselves and another illustration of how the adult world is "not with it." But if television is at all the wasteland that many critics of our culture think it is, young people finally need to see for themselves what life styles are being celebrated, where and what the phoniness is. Dare they avoid recognition of James Bond as "state's assassin"? Even though sponsors may say, "Well, somehow adolescents have to be emotionally prepared to participate in a cutthroat war civilization." What does a constant reiteration of this mode of being-in-the-world do to feeling sensitivities —even though we claim we don't take it seriously, but merely look at it for entertainment? Who is kidding whom? Or how have movies been able for at least thirty years to repeat ad nauseam the same type of central male hero—the cool, disconnected, family-and-heritage-alienated male who can wow them, love them, and then get up and leave with no thought of further connections or responsibility? What happens when this is the model of manhood presented for years and years in the entertainment world? Must we identify it for what it is, and ask, "Is this the picture of desirable man *we* interiorize? that women will have to marry?" What image as to what a woman must be if she is to survive in this world comes through the songs and shows of radio and TV? If you want to find out—and if you want to meet an anxious, fear-driven group—meet the wives of the rising young executives of a commercial masscomm civilization.

Let us catch the image-makers in the act, so that our society will no longer be victimized by them.

And when they do a good job, let us use masscomm to store in our persons wider ranges of experience put into compellingly striking image than we could ever hope to have just by ourselves.

Intent

In this chapter, I have been suggesting for a youth center of world life, activities which together might be called "young people and world culture." By "culture" meaning the symbols by which men live *together*. By "culture" also meaning style, quality, and content of consciousness and intersubjectivity.

Young people themselves should help create their culture, rather than have it sold to them.

Primarily, I have said, "Take seriously the new mode of mind and emotion and consciousness that is moving in man today. It is in its formative stage. Get into the act, influence it, shape it."

7. Sharpen a Few Ideas and a Picture of the Emerging World

Young people need places and occasions where they can bring to focus some very few elemental ideas that shape a world and a human life.

They don't have to have a *lot* of ideas. After all, there are not very many live, kicking ideas in the world. There are fewer *useful* ones. Schools, colleges, pretend that there are lots of them, but there are very, very few ideas that shape any one moment of mankind.

So we say to each other, "Center down into depth of understanding just a few elemental ideas. Go directly to originating thinkers who are contemporary. And to *original documents*— not third- and fourth-rate rewrites and explanations."

Martin Buber's "I-Thou" is one such very fundamental idea. If you follow Martin Heidegger's concept that the fundamental nature of a person is "an understanding potentiality-for-being," you find all kinds of implications. If you understand Victor Frankl's knowledge that the first and last freedom is the capacity to feel, then you have another insight fruitful all your life. If you should get hold of Bonhoeffer, you might have a theology for youth today. "Only in the midst of the world is Christ, Christ," is almost limitless in its productivity. So, also, "Christ taking form in a band of men."

A Ministry of Ideas

We have a special ministry of ideas and ideology to perform with juniors and seniors in high school and with young adults. Just about the time young people get up to the level where they have mind enough, education enough, experience enough, and an increasing awareness of need to really get hold of something, we fail them. We lose them. We underrate them. We reduce them all to the level of mediocrity. We keep them permanently children in their religious understanding. We have failed the intelligent young people of our churches.

Young people have the impression that we ourselves don't have much use for religious knowledge or ideas of religious import. They have the impression that we are anxiously smiling, hoping to be accepted as their friends, trying to find out how they feel, trying to imitate the jargon of the far-out in-group. But we do not have any set of ideas or convictions that make a difference in the ways we feel and handle the world. Young people have a lot of contempt for many adult youth leaders and ministers of churches. Often the contempt is voiced this way: "There is no point in talking to them because they don't know anything."

This is connected with the other judgment many of them have about all adults: "Adults have given no evidence that they know how to run the world, so why should we listen to them anyway!" It is not clear to them that we have sharp ideas that take account of the necessary facts and can be connected to produce events today. They feel that we are not with it, are not aware of the changes that are happening and will happen. They suspect us of trying (or pretending) to live in Old Time, rather than in New Time. Of which one evidence is that when we talk the religious, we use a language that comes out of the Victorian age (only the literary crust at that), rather than the images and words people actually use today in understanding life, in choosing at crossroads, in making a case with one's contemporaries.

Before high school seniors leave for college or work, they ought to have hold of a few ideas they can handle life with. And this can't just be given to them—they have to hammer them out in fierce searching conversation with their own peers. With a guarantor, catalyst, enabler, present. The group must be small enough that intense conversation can go on, and that experiencing can be mixed in with the ideas.

There are young people in every community and church who are going to be the leaders of civilization. We don't know who they are, but we can bring together a core of potentials. And help them become very *able* people who can put together worlds that have life-enhancing qualities. Become skilled in communication, arting, existence clarification, accustomed to risky giving of life. They will also have to have some Christian ideas. But how?

One helpful method of enabling some young people to architect the structure of a few central ideas—and the relationship of these ideas to each other and to lived moments—is the seminar.

The seminar is limited to six to eight members, meeting once a week for an hour and fifteen minutes. They know they are going to talk over ideas in connection with the crucial experiences they have had. And that they are going to try to make sense out of them. They are not meeting for a nice social time and gossip. It is not a therapy group trying to solve their problems with their parents—although such problems may come in. It is an attempt to develop some *structures for life*. To *architect a con-*

sciousness that will have resources and toughness to solve problems and enjoy life. Ideas are not just for the sake of solving problems, but for opening up life. And cohering it.

Sometimes the conversation begins with an idea they felt at the last meeting they wanted to pursue this time. Sometimes the group begins with an experience one of them has had that day. But however it begins, the focus is upon comprehending *ideas-in-situation*. There is no sequence-schedule of things to be considered for any particular meeting. But the adult leader has a cluster of ideas that he considers significant, and some precise richness of sub-ideas and lived moments that make each of these ideas sing with power. So exciting conversation can go on about an idea whenever its moment of timeliness arrives in the seminar. The conversation is a mode of theologizing which gets ideas and the preconscious interfused into one integrity.

For the youth doing this, it becomes transforming. They come back from college and say, "Taking part in the seminar group gave me something to live with. I can handle what is going on; I have some beliefs from which I can digest my studies." Life was put together for them in a situation where they could talk ideas in relation to the fundamental experiences they were having. Their deep hunger to get hold of some sharp ideas that make a difference was fed.

It is for us to expose them to the best ideas of the sharpest contemporary figures—the people in our day who are doing some real thinking. Ideas from merely the long, long ago are like dead fish on the beach for young people.

And instead of ourselves trying to say what these present frontiersmen are fermenting, let's get to young people the frontiersmen's original documents—how they said it. We have often mimeographed eight to ten pages collated from a person's writing —such as from Kierkegaard's polemic against conventional Christianity in his *Training in Christianity,* which each member reads before coming to the meeting.

A crucial quality of a seminar is to have continuous participation—members must agree that this meeting has priority over any other. Also, the length of time is important. Fifty minutes is not enough. And in the design as we have developed it, a weekend is scheduled about every three months where they have a day and a half to pursue some idea in greater depth. In one summer situation, each time they met one of them presented a four-page "position paper" on some idea crucial to him. In the course of the summer, they tried to develop a theology for youth. It was an ambitious project, but they did a lot of thinking and some very good thinking.

Also, a class that consecutively sets out to develop a system of life philosophy and a line of thought is back with us. With fast-moving, hard-hitting, depth-driving thought process. That no such course is allowed in the high school curriculum is an indication of how the leaders of American culture insist on trivializing young people.

For such a class, the teacher does not lecture all the time, but he is not afraid of presenting a model of some person's thought for the discussion to be about. And then he enables group thinking—being somewhat merciless, as a good surgeon, toward intentionally fuzzy and evasive talk. The one rule is "Be honest— don't pretend to think and feel what you don't. Don't hide and play games with us." The original documents considered include those that voice well current questionings and disagreements with traditional religious positions—often voicing more doubts than the young people have yet thought of. And through it all, moving toward stark honesty about how it is, at present, with the people in the discussing group. From time to time a class member presents a paper laying out his experience and what meaning he can offer from it.

These two are special forms of a *ministry of meanings*.[1] Meanings ministry is a major form of the church's ministry to

[1] See "Ministry of Meanings," a publication of the Youth Department of the World Council of Churches. *Risk*, Vol. I, Nos. 3 and 4, third and fourth quarters, 1965.

civilization. We are not trying to implant in people inert ideas and safely dead history, but we are trying to help them understand an immediacy with which they must deal, sense a possibility which expands, enlivens, opens up space for their living.

The crucial thing in all efforts is to select a few most significant ideas and go to the contemporary originating thinkers. But who are these people? You'll have to pick them out yourselves, because you can't do this kind of intensive work unless the "originative ones" are terribly meaningful to you. You must not try to enlist young people in ideas that don't speak to you.

We are discovering that Dietrich Bonhoeffer is a useful man. He worked out fresh theological thinking *with his life*. He didn't just read somebody's book or write a book of theology. He is a root of life, for he didn't get to finish his thinking. You have to imagine; you have to go on with it and see where it will take you. You have to do theologizing—discovering and conjecturing and mixing feeling and imaging and risking with the best that men have made of life. Out of such theologizing emerges a thrust and a momentum that brings freshness to the people of our times and the church.

The Great Words Have Been Trivialized

The great Christian experiences and the great Christian words need to be understood in much greater depth, understanding, and passion than the present generation of church members understands them. If the young people of our day don't understand them better than the present adults do, it is going to be a sorry world and a sorry church.

The great words of Christianity have become so trivialized and so "surfacized" in our time that they hardly have any power to awaken energies in people. They slip right through people's minds without anything ever being started in motion.

It's a *real hazard* to use the word "love" to a group of young people today. If you were to talk about love to a high school assembly, you would hear snickers from all over the room, audible enough to make you know that the word "love" has been taken over by the entertainment celebrities of our time and by the new morality. Love means success at making out with a girl, the beach love-in, the sex-ski weekend.

Love is offering a flower to a policeman as he is desperately trying to handle a difficult situation. (Probably a supreme act of arrogant imperviousness, rather than bearing his cross.)

The sermons that we preach seem to make love such an utterly impossible thing—so way up above us someplace that nobody in his right mind could assume that what is being said is going on in *actual life*.

Youth's difficulties in understanding love also come from parents. Too many boys and girls are caught in what is called the "communication bind"—having a well educated, attractive mother who plays it cool, who pretends to love the child and teen-ager deeply, and in the next moment tells him in devious ways that he is worthless and incompetent. He is always getting *conflicting signals* from her. How can he possibly *understand* what love can be when he gets such conflicting signals from the *same person?* And then there is the father who becomes emotional divorced from the mother so that the child senses that even though both his mother and father talk about how much they love each other, underneath it all bitter war is going on. Finally it all ends in the total coolness of a father and mother who are emotionally divorced from each other and both enjoying "cutting each other down to size." How can teen-agers possibly know what love is with all of that going on?

Consider also the considerable number of teens in the great cities who do not even know who their father is, and know a man primarily as one who every so often invades the home and has sexual relations with the mother. And for them—as for the tired, defeated businessman—sex is the one arena of proving they are, after all, men. What can they do with the word love?

Yet love is a word that points to the deepest mysteries and

meanings of life. How are you going to call up these deepest meanings and mysteries so that young people feel with some confidence that there is such a thing as *love* in this world?

We must come clear with a fundamental Christian interpretation of the meaning of sexual intercourse.

What is going on—really? Not just biology. "Fully sex" intercourse is an act of personal relationships, a fundamental art expression of oneself. It has something to do with a way of living with people in truth and fidelity.

We need to provide persons who want to make the good try at life with some ways of interpreting sex, so that they are not wholly at the mercy of the most vocal and high-pressuring people around them. A young person today has to have a philosophy about sex, so that he doesn't have to be open to everything and doesn't yield to "now" as the only imperative in life. Many recommendations in popular magazines and peer culture are subsexual. It is not sexuality that they are talking about. They are talking about dissociated sex—sex as dissociated from love, sex as a game and status point in an affluent war society, sex as disjointed "art happenings" that must not lead into growing meaning.

Spontaneity, freedom, openness are words in wide circulation today. And they are excellent words. But, as used, they all too often are diffuse, muddied in content, slippery in purpose. And result in destroying what they properly point to.

"Be open to new experience" too often means "Do what I want you to do even if it violates your integrity." Too often "openness people" think that openness means that one action in a situation is just as good as any other action could be, one need never stand up and fight, everybody should be allowed to live as he pleases out of his immediate feeling. The model of life is the movie and TV show where the scriptwriter can connect any consequences he wants to any action, and the more schizoid and absurd the sequence, the better the game he is playing with the spectator. Which is all right for a script, but not a very accurate guide to realistic expectations or humane development. Like all other values, openness must be held in conjunction with a zeal to enhance one's own integrity. It cannot mean having no self-identity, or no long-term engagement in bringing something off.

Openness is really the residue of a number of processes of living—not a character trait which one sets up as an ideal. Such processes as being free enough of self anxieties as to deeply care about other people, be understandingly sensitive to the existence situation of other persons. But not blurring oneself into them. Openness also comes from an inventive approach to what is before one—"O.K. This is what happened. So what do I do now to bring out new desirable possibility?" Openness is willingness to develop, as contrasted with willingness to flip with each blip.

Spontaneity, freedom, openness are all connected together. A surface interpretation defeats them all. As does failure to keep them acting together with fidelity to some persons, some causes, some developing enterprises. (It takes a long pull to bring off a significant enterprise.) By themselves alone, spontaneity, freedom, openness are not absolute values. If we saw them that way we would be moralists and fanatics. Always they are part of a *field of values*—which also includes at least the drive for meaning and responsibility.

They are also not absolutes, because it is impossible to be absolutely open. For every openness is a saying no to many other possibilities, is always a selected out limitation we put on present experience, is always a closing of doors to some consequences. Further, every experience leaves its residue which enables or disables our capacity to be.

And freedom is not being the eternal dilettante, but involves acquiring the skills and devotion to an art or profession that are necessary if one is to experience *"I am able,"* and anchorage for his identity. Freedom means—among other things—"I am able to do what I want to do." I have never mastered the piano, and that is my lack of freedom musically. No skills—no leading on into new horizons, no opening of new possibility.

Another word full of meaning is "phony."

It's what too many adults are! And too many young people who project their hatred and dissatisfaction of themselves upon "what awful parents I have. They made me what I am today."

"Playing games" is a version of phoniness. But "playing games" is ultimately unsatisfying. For lives in process of growing into unknowable futures hunger to be real, to be authentic, to find a truth which they dependably are. Who knows what constitutes a *human* being, and how you become the real article? Let's be about putting together a workable cluster of ideas on what it means to be *person,* so that we can be on our way.

With What Words Can We Organize Experience and Communicate?

Words such as spontaneity, freedom, openness, authentic, and phony are timely. And are worthy of much effort to establish what they can mean to us. For all our lives—in some degree—we will be moving from the familiar to the unknown.

Working on such "living concepts" will be where much of the good theologizing by young people will take place. For they will be firming up and using religious insight to see into the depths and structures of existence. And for the sake of *living by what they discover*—rather than using theology as a word game played on Sundays in Sunday morning language while in classes. They will learn to theologize in the thick of life. And in doing so will probably be inventing new words to do it with.

In the days of my grandfather—certainly in my great grand-parents' time—the language they fought, decided, and chose with was the language of the Bible. This is still true of some people today. But in many places it is decreasingly true. If the Christian faith is to influence people's choices and decisions, we have to put it into words that people use when they are choosing and deciding. I doubt if many contemporary businessmen choose and decide with words such as "reconciliation," or "atonement." Or with any other fourth- to nineteenth-century words that we use in church. The same thing is true for young people.

At a conference of three hundred adult leaders of youth—both Protestant and Catholic—held in 1965 in Minnesota there was almost unanimous agreement in checking as "very true" this item—

"The great words of the church are not the words that young people whom I know use to choose and think with."

So we better translate the great words into words and imagery that young people can use to choose and feel with. And demonstrate that the words are usable—more so than any others —in the difficult situations of life.

For nobody understands a word—or makes it one of his "speaking words"—unless the word has been used in situations that are important to him. How does a child (or anybody) learn the meaning of a word? He learns it as the "utterance occasion" of someone significant to him. A little child hears his mother and father talking, and he hears them use certain words. He begins to imitate the words; he accidentally uses the word in the right situation and he gets "Ohs" and "Ahs." So he gets a glimmer of the meaning of the word. Then he begins to use the word in his own expressive spontaneity and to speak it in the kind of situation in which he ought to use it. He doesn't sit down at the dictionary and learn words. He really never learns the meaning of a word when mother and father sit down and try to "teach it to" him. He has to hear the word *in situation*. (This is what is meant by "utterance occasion.") And then *he* has to use it in situations and have people recognize what he is talking about.

Young people have to learn to use theology by hearing people use its words when they are struggling with life. They have to learn to use the great words of Christianity by hearing people use them as they talk about current events. As they are in the process of trying to make sense out of "what happened to me

101

today?" *The word* has to be used in *situations!* The dictionary definitions, and the great originating occasions when they were used with powerful effect, are helpful *after* this has happened.

Young people often get the impression from their confirmation classes that we think we know all there is to know about theology (or that we *really* understand none of the words we use). And that all they can do is to memorize the theology package we give them. There is little recognition in confirmation classes that there is theologizing still to be done—particularly right now. That we do theologizing for the sake of becoming life world rather than death world, for the sake of communion with God and fellow man in the particular habitat we inhabit.

The biblical records and the realities are still with us—our job is to make fresh formulations and create fresh awareness. But even more importantly, in confirmation activities, young people should prove that they are fit to join an enterprise setting out through time toward a destiny; that they have an existential grasp of the new which God is offering in their moment of history-making; that they have at least one truth and bit of good news which they can offer people about them.

If we could only change confirmation classes to get in just a glimmer of this kind of theologizing, young people might not leave the church in such droves after they are confirmed. Young people would begin to say, "This is a living God that we have to deal with."

And we are in the midst of fresh theologizing about the nature of God and the originative myth by which we live.

Take Dietrich Bonhoeffer's assertion, "Only in the midst of the world is Christ, Christ," and see what that does to your theology and picture of the kind of world this is to live in. Ask yourself his question, "Where in the world is Christ suffering at the hands of an evil world?" and then put yourself in the midst of that place, participate in that suffering in a transforming way. And you will be doing the kind of fresh theologizing which is recovering the original impetus in Christianity.

As I understand Bonhoeffer, he is saying that if you situate yourself any place else, you will never be able to discover the reality of Christ. I also understand him to say that you have to get rid of the image of Christ sitting up in heaven on the right hand of God the Father Almighty, with this earth in the charge of his deputies—a pope, the ministers, the powerful on earth. This isn't any kind of theology for our times! Christians have always had the doctrine of the *living* Christ. We have always had the doctrine of the Holy Spirit. Of religious reality as process, rather than idol.

Bonhoeffer helps us see that Christ is that particular form of life in which the evil and incompletenesses of the world are held within the love and creativeness of God.

And therefore there are not *two* realms—the realm of ideas and the realm of action, a sacred world and a secular world, the church and the world. There is only one realm—the realm of Christ! Which is a realm not of perfection, but of struggle. Not a finished product, but a continual outbreak of both evil and good. A realm where the actualities of alienation and rebellion from reality are present and have to be overcome in their time by each generation.

A Time of Choosing Life Myth and Ideology

Today's young people—as all men through time—need a central credible story of how new life once originated and is constantly originating. Of how what now is, is being transformed into new possibility—of how hate and brutality have been out-wearied and overcome, chaos given significant form, despair changed into hope, adhesion to Old Time given up for expectancy toward the ever-coming God who makes all things new.

A young person requires a flood of news about where this is happening in his contemporary world. He needs to relive vividly the most striking of such events in the history of what he regards as "my people Israel." In faith, he must project the essential plot as possibility here and now for his one life on earth. He must grasp in three dimensioned vision (past-present-future) some believable-for-him drama of how life originates.

For, as a *human* being, a person is never totally imprisoned in a "now" which is merely the pushes and pulls of an unaware environment. He lives and moves and has his being in the meaningful possibility which only a human consciousness constitutes for itself.

And so he requires a religious myth that illuminates the events and the potential of his life. And that of his people as they face the historical decisions of their time in mankind.

Myth does not mean a fanciful story made up in some time of ignorance and superstition, but a dramatic image insight into the innermost moving—the story within the story—of the making of mankind.

Man has no choice whether he has and uses such a myth. For he cannot participate in his civilization without picking up some myths. He cannot expose himself to newscasts; read newspapers, comic strips, magazines; invite TV and advertisers into his home without whirling myths entering and overcoming his mind. His only choice is which myths will become his pivotal ones. Within which heritage and tradition—of long or short length—does he believe he finds ecstatic life?

In choosing his originating life myth, he chooses a dramatic plot which he invites to form his life. And at the same time he is choosing his troth—a relationship he is true to over a period of time.

Today we have arrived at the point in history-making when the choice of determinative life myth is almost overwhelmingly fateful. Shall we continue with the false myth that the *white* man was meant to have dominion over the earth, and all other people are more distant from God? Or that God is at work in the world only where Christians are? That the originating source of LIFE is porno-violence? That the rights of man originate with the whims and prejudices of national legislatures? That

104

technical competence makes the man? Or, at least, that financial wizardry does? That playing it cool is realization of the warmth of being human?

In his book *Uncommitted,* Kenneth Keniston points out that for years and years, the myths and images presented in American literature, art, movies, TV unfit us to be *human* beings—

> Few would deny that ours is a time whose most visible public myths are negative, deterrent, even satanic.
>
> The implicit message, repeated a thousand times over, is that excitement, glamour, passion, and fascination, all inhere in the negative and the forbidden.
>
> By removing imagination from contact with everyday reality, we deprive our daily existence of any conscious link with the non-cognitive, affective, and symbolic stratum which might otherwise support and enrich it.
>
> Evil always has its seductiveness, but when good has been deprived of adventure, poetry, excitement, the fascination of the demonic becomes almost overwhelming.[2]

A major enterprise of exploring, judging, choosing fundamental myth must be mounted in our time. For both adults and young people. This is perhaps our major educational effort. Just this and that good idea, or helpful advice, is almost totally inadequate. Young people today stand at the point of *great* and *large* choices—for or against civilizing man. Only a *pattern* of idea rather than an isolated idea, a *totalizing feeling and mind image-myth,* rather than abstract intellectualism, can move us, can hold together the total complexity which the world is and which we are.

It remains to emphasize that a "myth of all origination of life" can center on how the *person* comes into being, can be transformed, can be an originating center. But the larger myth is

[2] *The Uncommitted: Alienated Youth in American Society* (New York: Dell, 1967).

also the story of how *a People* came into existence—the People setting out through time toward a destiny which is "my people, Israel." The venture in history-making, the life style, which is also my fate and destiny. The "dream, mighty of wings" which is a *communal* fact.

Too often, the church has centered upon the myth of how the purely personal and private life originates. Upon the possible drama of the inner-personal region. And this must never be lost.

But in a time of making a new world—which is now upon us—we need equally to hold up a viable myth of *history-making.* Of how a people—a world-embracing people where each man hears good news in his own language—is originated.

Erik Erikson calls this an ideology—a vision of the new that is trying to be born in this very moment of history-making. As he has seen human life, such a vision becomes a young person's "second mother"—birthing him into a life of generativity, identity, and integrity.

Within religious conviction, an ideology is an imagination-stirring statement of new potential which God is offering man in the history-making *now* upon us. And man's yes or no, his stupid insistence upon living in Old Time rather than in New Time, his sensitivity to God's new, his "choose you this day whom you will serve; but as for me and my house, we will serve the Lord"—all these make a difference in that history-making. All these destroy or flower other people, the community, the person making the choice. The choice is therefore not to be made lightly or inadvisedly. It is most difficult.

This kind of ideology is a prophetic voicing of a narrow pass through which humanity is now going. It speaks of a direction in some forking of the roads which mankind must take. Of what kind of people with what kinds of disciplines and competency are needed for leadership. It defines some point of strategic breakthrough and some battles that have to be won. Once more it points out the immemorial enemies of mankind, but particularly those at this instant. It puts people on a high tableland from which they see a Promised Land and a Journey.

An ideology is "this instant in history theologizing."

And no youth, no youth program, no center of world youth culture can avoid working at it.

8. Participate in the Passion and Action of Our Times

World events put to each "destiny generation" of young people a particular problem-opportunity they must be particularly relevant to. Some threat of devastating destruction, some new possibility for good is timely to *them*.

The Elvis Presley generation had to make up their minds not to conform to—or to slide into—the Presley style of existence. The flux of history gave the Korean war generation of youth its central questions to handle. The depression of the nineteen-thirties gave many young people a searing fate; for just when their developmental life task was to make their way into an adult world, the world apparently didn't want them and had no place for them.

To another generation, the problem-opportunity is freedom and equal relationship for both negro and white. To keep in relationship and communication with each other while the black man builds up power. Or perhaps it is a whole complex which would include what to do with the horrible inner city of American cities; how to plan and bring into being a megalopolis fit for human beings. It would include revolutions all over the world in who controls civilization and toward what directions. And is terrorism the final answer—both to upset and to control?

But another problem-opportunity which is not so sharply put—because few are effectively equipped to make an issue of it—is the one with which this book began. A primary staging area of young life is the emergence of a new mode of human consciousness clear across the world. Because of electronic communications, man's mind and emotions and seeing are attached to the world in a new way and with a new universalism and simultaneity. And in the long run this change in style of communication produces a new explosion of man.

Since present young people are the first generation who all their lives have been living with this new mode, one of their major destinies is to shape it; influence the quality of electronic mass communications; maximize its tremendous potential to create a world ecumene and world history-making and to symbolize the depths of the human psyche. The emergence of a world youth culture is one evidence of the promise which is today's youth's to realize. This is one arena of passion and action of their times in which youth is already immersed as a major consumer and creator.

The particular fate-opportunity of a new destiny generation is, of course, open to all living at that time—both adults and youth. And all must work on meeting it. But since it comes at a young person at the time when he must find his niche in the scheme of things and begin to form worlds with his generativity, it comes with a peculiarly *forming* intensity. His generation cannot avoid bearing its stigmata.

Justice Holmes' advice comes to each generation, as well as

his own: We must participate in the passion and action of our times, at peril otherwise of being judged not to have lived.

Many young people, like many adults, prefer the risk of never living. And all young people (and the rest of us) are not particularly impressed with what present adults have done about history-making. Even though they have survived more shocks and changes than perhaps any other generation ever experienced.

The many young people who hunger to participate in passion and action should be enabled.

So one of the growing edges of any youth program today is to switch from a guiding image of young people as a "pleasant joe" mutual admiration society and as people to be ministered unto and nurtured. Switch to Justice Holmes' memorable image. And enable them to find ways that they can take part in the fate, the feeling, the suffering consequences of some class of people *other than their own*. Enable them to be civilization-builders.

And do this at the same time that some frontier adults are also engaged in such enterprises. Always there has to be an over-lap of *some* of each generation. The other alternative is to kill off—in one way or another—a whole generation. And sometimes it is the adult, sometimes the youth generation. There are many ways of murdering people. Particularly individuals who are alone.

But what would be the lived moments of a youth center which encourages and enables young people to participate in the "go," the richness of feeling and conviction of some history-making in the time of their life?

The Primacy of Being Places and of Firsthand Seeing-feeling

New life—and risky life—does not begin with new loads of ver-balized ideas, but from *perception*. From head-on seeing some-thing with which we have to do. From new perception of our-self-in-world, of life world-for-us.

110

So we invent a program of going places and being where action is occurring at some crossroads of encountering significant environment.

This can result in even more imperviousness and narrower minds than we started with. The world traveler is sometimes the greatest snob, the least moved by human suffering! The reason is the *attitude with which he sees*. Our perception (seeing and feeling what is there) is quite different when we are present as one hoping to be entertained, hoping to have our eliteness confirmed, remaining cool and aloof as a visiting spectator and judge, than when we are present as one feeling *with* the situation and its people, so that our fortune and identity are also at stake in the outcome of the struggle.

So we must add the element of *experiencing* to any program of more extensive perceiving. Both of them together are exactly what young people would like to have. And are the foundations of any growth program.

Enlarging the area of experiencing checks with what we have already talked about—the lived moment. Young people need more lived moments and more accurate perceptions coming out of them. John Dewey—the man who let loose the concept of experience as the basis of all education—finally made a definition of *religious experience* which states exactly what we are reaching for here. For Dewey, religious experience was inserting your life into some bend of events and trying to make something better become real in that situation, willing to suffer the consequences and stick to it with tenacity even in the face of suffering.

And such is what we mean by developing a lively program of experiencing with and for young people.

Everybody today has more information and sensations coming at him than he can possibly process. Think of being tuned into mass communications for three, four, five hours a day (as many young people are), in addition to all the books they're supposed to read in school, and then ask if you think a teen-ager needs another load of secondhand information thrust into him.

He needs a program of first-hand perceiving—of actually being *present*. And a range of religious experiencings of giving himself without reservation into the transforming and creating of some bit of world.

A student once said to me after his first month at seminary, "I passed all the examinations in college with flying colors, but I discover as I look back now that I don't remember a single thing of all I studied. And I'm getting scared, for the same thing is beginning to happen to me here. How am I going to get so I can remember something?" We finally decided that he must get some experiences so that he could organize and remember what was important. For up to that time, he had had no experiences vivid enough to organize *him*. Particularly new experiencings of *himself*.

Maybe young people (and their parents) are so unable to learn Christianity because they have not had enough vivid experiences.

If we hope to vitalize or revitalize any group, we begin by enlarging their area of experience.

Placing One's Self

So we come to the question, "How embark upon a program of seeing, sensing, experiencing with a group of young people? Where are such experiences available?" Obviously this will always be specific to the particular time and community which is this group's available world—the *nearest Thous* that can be dialogued and created with. So nobody can decide what it is for any other person or group. We can only set some guide questions. If any one of them can be followed through, significant living begins.

Before we state the questions, let's agree on one ground rule for this particular pursuit. While it's true that such experiencing happens *wherever* people really meet and have to do with each other, let's think now exclusively of places and situations *outside* the four walls of a classroom. Let's add also the dimension that the situation we're going to see and act into has something significant to do with "participating in the passion and action of our times." That it is a *place where* the shape and vitality of some institution, the answering of some question put to our destiny generation, the coming of new life into civilization, can be seen— even though faintly. We are out for big game—though in our own territory.

How do you go about deciding where to situate your life so that things will begin to happen to you? Where you will get wakened? Where your life could cause things to happen and be part of cumulating consequences?

Question 1. Where—in the world available to you—is human dignity expressing itself? Where is it creating something that ought to have a chance?

> Human dignity is someone (preferably a group of someones) refusing to be a worm—to be walked over, used, played games with, not listened to, treated as part of the furniture of the world, not allowed to participate in forming the society in which they live.

> Human dignity is people standing up to fight injustice, when they are likely to get hurt.

> Human dignity is the courage to be. To be expressive rather than defensive. To be able to "take it" and not be overcome by others' hatreds and evil at loose in the world.

> Human dignity is imagination believing there is a future when everything looks dark and very difficult. The capacity to hope when ordinary men are in despair.

> Human dignity is creativeness freshly coming into significant form. When something new that hasn't been in this situation before is opening up and you are helping it happen.

113

It's forthright fun to be a human dignity. Where would we go to be part of it happening? How would we get into the act?

Question 2. Where is "the real man" suffering at the hands of an evil world?

Where is love being profaned and violated? People left lonely and alienated? Hate and indifference sanctioned and affirmed as a way of life? War as the joyful policy of a nation?

Where does arrogance have dominion? Where are lies and blurry half-truths substituted for the truth; idolatry for the religious? What power structures have to be shook up and brought to task?

Where are the persons whose development you and your kind of people are thwarting—at least trying to ignore, passing by "on the other side" rather than on their side?

Where is the "childhood" of a new future being pushed in the face, the rising of new life from defeat being stomped on, the transformation of what is into something better being despised and rejected? (For Christ is a transforming and transmuting at work in the world, not just a picking up of people who have fallen among thieves.)

"Where is Christ suffering at the hands of an evil world?" is a Bonhoeffer question which he answered with his own life. For the sequel is "Put yourself at that crossroads." Bonhoeffer's life guarantees that there will be enough to happen to you that you won't be living lukewarmly anymore—or thinking little thoughts.

Question 3. Where is the love of God and man toward man breaking out in power? The revitalization of a civilization begins with a surge of tremendous feeling; a new person begins with a tremendous surge of love. Is this happening anywhere?

The great days of Christianity have been marked by the outbreaking of love. This was the forming experience of Paul's, of Martin Luther's, of John Wesley's days—to mention but three times in history. Could today be such a time—or the prelude to such a time—or the end?

Question 4. What new *possibility of history-making* is being offered now?

Then you could insert your life in that bend of history-making. And your life would begin to count. The effects of your life would go on even past your own three score years and ten. Because you'd be throwing it into something that is not just your own individual gain, but something that man and God are bringing forth now. You'd meet intense people, and the fellowship would be binding.

All these questions emphasize, "Brother, *you* can't live in the past." You yourself can no longer walk around the walls of Jericho blowing trumpets. The Hebrews did that. That was their moment of history-making. You can read the Bible and get the story of the fallen walls of Jericho, but you have to find *your* Jericho to walk around and blow trumpets against and risk yourself. You no longer can be living in Egypt, hearing the call of Moses to come out into the wilderness toward a promised land. You can't live off his victory, although you can profit by it. You have to ask, "What exodus is God calling for today?" And will you hear the call and begin to move? As our Jewish friends say, the Passover occurs whenever the convinced Jew moves out of bondage into freedom. He has to find *his* situation in which he must move from enslavement to freedom. Unless he himself moves from bondage today, he is not participating in the Exodus.

Intent

These are the questions which every *human* being today answers somehow or other, whether he knows it or not. Where they lead us, we never know. But that is just what makes them so important. Questions whose answers we already know are not worth our attention. But these are major questions about which we should talk when planning a youth program. And when we are individually exploring where we can place our one life on earth.

If you and your young people embarked on an intensive program of perceiving and experiencing, participating in the passion and action of the times, what would you do? Where could you begin?

We cannot respect ourselves if we run out on the action of our time in history. And there is no way to effectively carry out the cry, "Stop the world, I want to get off." Except the illusory one of drugging one's self. But more importantly, it is in the very midst of struggle (unless our attention is solely upon our opponents and upon winning) that the depth of persons shines through. And we are proud to know them, proud of being a human being. For we ourselves may not be much, but the cause we serve is great—and right. Our lives are not planless, meaningless, normless, solitary, sanctionless anomie.

It may be that we are at the beginning of an exciting surge forward in the experiment of mankind. These years may be the beginning of great vitality in the church. A rather monumental evolution is going on that's leading us away from a merely conventional Christianity. An evolution that believes that a God who revealed himself only once would not only be irrelevant but uninteresting. That creation is *continuing*.

Because of God, *you are able to* love the world. Because of God, you can be a truth. You were not meant to be a nonentity. You can't do apart from him, but you yourself are meant to do something and to be a particular person. To exist as passion and action.

116

9. The Inner-personal

The inner-personal region where the self lives is a tumultuous lake of anxieties, doubts, despairs, resentments, hatreds, acute estrangements, guilts, brokenness, powerlessness—in violent combat with their opposites, the heaves and tides of loves and warm belongings, horizoned futures, hopes and destinies, conviction, life energies making good and causing things to happen, fulfillments, celebration.

This tumultuous lake is constantly windswept and rain-whipped. Contemporary young people have hurled at them a constant rain of porno-violence via masscomm and world daily events, mixed with the slick consumption of an affluent society. What human consciousness can survive such pollution mixed with other inputs?

If we were to analyze this inner-personal region into its functioning components, we might list—

1) self-consciousness;

2) the intentional arc which puts things together into possible futures;
3) the arena where decision goes on, where governance has its home;
4) the room of inner speech—which presents, explores, invents, and metaphors;
5) the inner population of people we respect. And will risk for.

Forms of I Am

The major organizer of self-consciousness is *I am* (I experience myself)—*I am able, I am desirable, I am connected with something that is true to me.* Thus being a person is to experience that one feels intensely and is caring about what happens. Able to say to himself, "I am here. I am the person responsible for some of it. This is me."

He needs to experience new awakenings of aliveness, undergo the surge of exciting thought. To sense, "This is my coming-out party."

In brief, to experience himself as a *subject* participating in its own becoming and with depth of further potential.

Sometimes the young person becomes so numbed with futility that he is unable to see or feel himself. His productive healthy self becomes unavailable, and he is left with access to only an angry, resentful self, a defensive self set back on its heels, a stupid self. Sometimes a raw flood of sensations overwhelms his power to organize his consciousness. Sometimes he feels that he is a finished puppet jerked into this and that motion by strange forces inside himself. And at times he does things that cause him to feel alien to himself, estranged, separated by an impassable gulf from his own vital core, no longer a friend of himself, no longer able to transform what is.

Such times can be an almost total disintegration or the emergence of striking realization that *I am.* Not a god—all-

118

wise, all-loving, all-powerful and successful—but a finite human being who does make mistakes, doesn't know it all, always has to struggle with conflicting impulses, with choices whose outcomes cannot be guaranteed, in a world resistant to his will and often cantankerously hell-bent for evil and destruction.

I am able is a confident form of *I am.* So that instead of running from situations and evading people, the person walks into life.

"I can handle life in a precarious world. I can think. I have an identity—I know somewhat what I am made of. I can place my life where the action is, test my powers against tough problems, bring myself off. I am able to make contact with the inwardness of other people and create with them. I'm on my way to being principled originality."

But the nagging question, "Am I desirable?" is always present. Always a young person is tasting the self that he is, and making judgments.

Sometimes he tastes good to himself; sometimes most repulsive, bitter, acrid. He experiences himself as guilty, as failure, as phony, as weak—and the taste spreads to cover the all of himself. At other times he tastes a truth that he is, or the warmth with which some person relates to him, and his *I am desirable* is confirmed.

Desirable, of course, does not mean perfect. And he has to learn that he is an ambiguous mixture of desirable and undesirable—without losing his capacity to taste the high quality when it is there.

Self-consciousness also reports, "I am connected with something that is true to me," or "I am horribly disconnected," or "There is nothing that is true to me. I have only quaggy swamp to walk on."

Always a young person feels rooted and connected, or falling headlong down bottomless nothingness, twisting and turning. He often experiences himself as a de-orbited astronaut in an encased capsule that tumbles over and over out of control, no longer able to successfully land on peopled earth.

He is disconnected when very little of his energies and love power is tendoned on to vitalities outside himself. When he feels alienated from the institutions of adult society. When all his life he has felt accepted only when he is the center of uncritical admiration. When he has had little experience of that kind of difference, disagreement, and conflict whose outcome is better relationships.

Like all the rest of the human race, a young person will do almost anything to escape from this catastrophic condition of no support and find some solid social ground on which he can walk. He wants to feel part of an intermingling web of people who believe in each other and in something together.

A center of contemporary culturing will invite, in many different ways, the young person to connect himself with something that is true to him, and to which he can be true.

The Intentional Arc

The human consciousness is power to organize worlds in which it can live. Even what we see is selected out and organized by our consciousness. It is as if all the powers of our body and mind were focused into one intentional arc which *groups* what is out there and puts it into significant form. (Much of the energies of that intentional arc are the consciousness of self that we have just spoken of—*I am, I am able, I am desirable, I am connected.*)

A peculiar nature of *human* consciousness is that it binds time together. The inner-personal region *is* a power that interweaves past-present-future into one story and possibility of journey. It is always busy doing this. It images futures—into which it gallops. It fills each present with a *fullness* of time—a richness of memories, contemporary experiencings, developing possibilities. It sets up projects and long-term stirrings which even a lifetime is too short to complete.

Always a young person senses himself as a *journey into existence*—or as a regressive retreat into a childhood community made by others. Always he senses himself as an incarnation of the process of becoming—or as the diffuseness of a not yet born or a refusal to be born.

Journey into existence is the life or death task of adolescence.

A journey into existence is a journey into becoming a *particular* something. And thus becoming manifest—to others and to oneself. A *particular* something is a dependable structure and centering. So that the person knows that he will not disintegrate and diffuse when faced with enmity and problem. That he can establish transactions with the necessary world and handle situations never before faced.

As contrasted with a trip—from which one returns to the place from which he started (having been a spectator and a consumer of sensations)—a journey is exploration and colonizing of new territory.

In the hero myth of all primitive tribes, journey means leaving the "village" where the battles and agonies and creation of life are done by others, and going out to prove oneself against the enemies of mankind. Journey means to fight in the times and places of future-coming, discovering love and destiny through engagement with the world. To establish some frontier outpost and hold it against all comers. Knowing that no one else can do this for him. And that there is no other way of becoming a *somebody* with distinctiveness and skills rather than another sponge or interchangeable part. There is no other way of becoming able to generate life.

Person-in-touch with God emerges only through participating in the sufferings and struggles of men in this world in such a way as to discover and initiate new vitality. Of course one suffers. May be defeated and frustrated. But he is not falling headlong down bottomless nothingness. He is on journey.

A center for young people and world culture is a place where future-past-present can be bound together in new ways. Where imaginative projections of new art, new humanity, new meanings can be journeyed.

The Decision Arena

And now to that aspect of the inner-personal which is the "studio" of this person as artist and architect of personal existence, home of self-governance, arena where decision is played out.

This inner-personal region is built by choosing and suffering the consequences. A robot can carry out commands, a computer can carry out programmed directions, and a "vidiot box" vibrates with programmed sensations. But only a human self is freedom to shape itself by its own decisions as it actively values what is and the possibilities it invents.

So the self is artist. Artist of personal existence. Of an inner-personal region. Of a self-in-world.

Each *person as self* is an artist that senses the innermost stirrings of both the world and the inner-personal region, captures them before they pass on into the abyss of the gone forever, clarifies their thrust and tune, puts them into enhancing juxtaposition with other patterns of beauty-meaning, keeps shaping them into significant forms.

Such arting and architecture work is high priority in any youth program of religious quality.

For each young person is this functioning artist—sensing, dreaming, shaping versions of himself. Not trying merely to defend himself and survive, but to actualize—to be the fullest human being he can be. And with style.

So the inner-personal region is also a governace system that rejects actions and designs of life that do not fit his style. It lines up choices so that they cumulate in value. The decision arena holds his journey on course so that he can better achieve the projects of his one life on earth.

Like all governance systems, the self of the decision arena region must be powerful enough to maintain a *system* of relationships and a momentum. Yet open enough to the burgeoning of new possibility that it can transcend what it already has achieved and leap into a new era without losing its basic identity.

Inner Speech

Looking at all these activities, we can see that the inner-personal region is a room always buzzing with inner speech.

For such activities require a great lot of talking back and forth with ourselves as well as with other people. Perhaps we have not paid enough attention to the importance of inner speech and how we can help it develop a rich language.

Inner speech is hardly ever in sentence structure. Sentences are something grammarians insist upon—partly for the good reason that more of the workings of the mind are then revealed. But when it is our own mind talking with our own consciousness, both already know the subject and object of the conversation. So they talk back and forth with "blobs of meaning"—with images and feeling pulses that have everything hidden in them before words have cut up the global meaning into parts that can be identified and combined in a new way. And when inner speech does consist of words, the words are largely prepositions, verbs, adjectives, phrases of relationship or alienation.

Most of our choosing and deciding, most of our sense of self-identity and how we feel about it, most of our feelings, most of our imaginative inventing and acting, most of our governance of ourselves and our relationships, most of our conscience work is done with inner speech.

We need to know more of its modes. We can start with the assumption that the great truths of a religious faith must incorporate themselves into the *inner speech* of people. Otherwise they will never actively enter into the deciding process, the coding of feelings and intentions, the imaginative invention and artistry which most fundamentally a consciousness is.

Inner Population of Significant Others

Much of the power of every person's inner-personal region is the population of people understood and valuings treasured.

Each person we meet is seen by us as a vortex of actions and potentials. Some are fascinating enough working models of a system of personal energies that we take these models into our make-up. This process is often called "identification"—we take their identity into our identity, and therefore to some degree our identity into theirs.

Hopefully we understand enough of their inner-personal that their *modes of being,* rather than just their surfaces, begin to reside in us and are available when we need it. Within our consciousness, these fascinating people are very alive images of desirable life. It is not just that we like them, but that they are powerfully and attractively human and so give us a shaping. They are life-for-us. They are within us as Significant Others with whom we carry on interior dialogue. Such an "identified with" person may become a life-long Significant Other. They are the people whom most of all we do not want to be separated from.

A young person is particularly fortunate who identifies with a small group of four or five people or an organized movement. A web of people who believe in each other and in something together, who invent together and awaken each other's aliveness and imagination.

This interiorized population makes the self powerful. But it also leads us to true self-forgetfulness (a de-centering of ourselves as the pivot of the universe). We begin to care about these people and what happens to them. We risk for them. We put out incredible amounts of energy in creative fidelity to their growth.

And so we are doubly empowered.

This Is Conscience

What we have been talking about in this chapter could be called "conscience." Taken together, the chapter is a new and more adequate concept of conscience than is usually abroad. Conscience is too often spoken of as an internalization of the demands and rejections of one's society. That is only a biting conscience. Further, conscience is so often thought of as a sort of entity which operates apart from the person as an enemy, spy, policeman. Whereas conscience *is the person* functioning in the ways we have been exploring.

Whatever it is called, strengthening, enriching, and arting of the inner-personal region is a major development to be brought off well during the adolescent years.

10. The Momentum and the Tune

The "go" of any center of young life is *hilaritas*. A prevailing *style of being* that has the tonus of a muscle in healthy performance. A fullness that is bringing off life, rather than impoverished moaning or demonic existence.

Hilaritas is a Latin word used for a number of centuries to refer to a certain quality of some people's lives which might be called "courage enjoying being a freedom." "Integrity" or "power which understands life" could be substituted for "courage," and the meaning would be the same.

Expressive Spontaneity

Hilaritas is expressive spontaneity. Doing the relevant thing because—at its own pace and quality—the wholeness of ourselves leaps up toward life. It is not acting out an impulse. It is not an

induced hilarity—i.e., that for which we first have to drug ourselves. It is not a surrender to the pressures of life. Such as indicated by the directions "This music happens to you. You have
to give yourself up to it, and let it take your mind."

Hilaritas is expressive of the person freely being himself. In
what he does is a personal signature, some distinctiveness that is a
hieroglyph of his name.

Everything about *hilaritas* is opposed to the assembly line
where everything must be done in a common way, and as defined
by those who are in charge. The opposite of *hilaritas* is the feeling
and thinking which are mere extensions of a transistor radio or
TV, authoritative person, or "the crowd." Where the good is felt
to be entirely outside oneself, and that one exists only when he is
plugged in, and his consciousness massaged into the electronic
and tribal beat.

Profound Confidence

Hilaritas is a lively confidence in one's own sensitivity, troth,
work. A vitalizing assurance that what one is doing will put forward growth in the world, even though the immediate society
does not approve.

Every great artist—painter, writer, statesman, architect of
his own life—must at times be able to disregard the judgment of
his peers and contemporaries because of profound confidence in
the rightness of his grasp of fundamental truth. This seems to be
an egotism, and it may easily become such. *Hilaritas* does involve
a willingness to be an aristocrat of the soul and a despiser of
mediocrity and crawling worms. So it includes a certain detach-
ment from, and invulnerability to, what other people think and
feel, what fashion or custom is, what has already been established. Plus a certain faith that a new becoming is due in the
world and something of its destiny is in one's hands.

Therefore our *hilaritas* must include within itself a necessary
quality of humor that enables us to stand off from ourselves—

and from what other people do to us—and look at what has been going on in perspective, seeing both our foibles and our achievements, and the part in relation to some whole. Seeing that the immediate difficulty is not the whole story of our life, that the wart on our face is not the whole definition of our contours. The present moment too will pass, and for him who lives as a man, the future may bring other possibilities. *Hilaritas* has built-in resilience.

Hilaritas is not necessarily loudly vocal. Some of our most intense moments of profound joy are quiet feelings of shalom—that we are being what we were meant to be, that we are immersed in the givens that make human beings. And that this good life is not something alien to us, an external command and demand upon us.

There is a rightness to things, and we are in right relations with its forming and shaping.

Shalom is living with a sense of the pulse of life. Of the mystery, moreness, wonders of existence. It is an expression in a finite human being of the fundamental graciousness deep within all life. A divine kind of abandon, an infinite generosity which flows and outgrows, rather than traveling the weary circle of self-reliance.

Sensitive to the Personal

We live in a mood of *hilaritas*, therefore, when we are able to enter into and receive the feelings and existence situation of other selves, inwardly affirming that they have the right to feel and to make decisions, trying to make sure that we sense the struggle to be person that is there. Being *for* the person, though we may disagree with his action, and may exercise some governance of the situation.

Over the long haul, we delight in such inter-subject existence for and with people we encounter.

128

A "Nevertheless"

Hilaritas-delight is something quite different from slap-happy, shutting-out-the-facts-of-life style of constricted consciousness and delusion by illusions. *Hilaritas* can come only from an expansion of awareness and of self. It is a quality of ourselves as life world in an actual world. *Hilaritas* is decidedly not identical with optimism, forced graciousness, carefully modulated voices, irreal people, restricted consciousness.

Hilaritas comes *after* we are aware of evil and defeat. We have conflicts and dark moments; but are not overcome by them. We suffer injustices and mistreatment but they do not become the focus of our continual attention. We too taste the terror and demonry of human living. We feel intensely anger, despair, joy—but we come through. The destruction, disintegration, alienation, determined stupidity, sloth that actually exist in world-available-to-us hit us, but do not have dominion. Even though we are mixed up with these disasters, they are not our idols, not our gods nor our masters. We feel and assert a "nevertheless." We may not win, but our life is not trapped and dehumanized. It sings a melody—it is a tune. We are transcendence, and live with expectancy that potential will break out into "something more."

If necessary, we go down fighting, having played the part of a man, asserting a *yes* rather than mere negativity, asserting our freedom to take an attitude toward what is happening even if we can't change the course of events at the moment.

D'Artagnan might be one image of *hilaritas*. Whomever the enemy and whatever the odds, he was an integrity which could not be profaned or conquered. Even though he might be killed, he would not die by his own fears or attempts to conform.

John Kennedy seemed to live *hilaritas*. And so people over the world felt that at last here was a man. A man who was for life. Not *naïvely*, but one "bred and born in a briar patch"—the thicket of events that man today has to live in.

St. Francis of Assisi lived with *hilaritas*—a sublime indif-

129

ference to the *things* of life, the worries for status and people's good opinions which dominated most people of his time. These he resolutely renounced, having found his "alleluia."

Jesus of Nazareth lived a profound indifference to what the rulers of his society thought of him. He was a profound self-confidence that he was meant to be in cahoots with God making man. And that this withness could be chosen, even when defeat became inevitable.

Intent

The quality of a youth center of world culture depends upon the presence of a core of youth and adults who *enjoy* being such selves-in-world. Young people and adults who set a pace of full living.

Such adults might be looked upon as guarantors that the life of *hilaritas*, shalom, belief in potential, is not a silly expectancy, nor does it end with youth. Also guarantors that *this particular* young person, whom they notice and talk with, being what he is, is worthy of respect and has a future.

So a center needs adults who are not looking for bad spots in young people's lives, trying to rub their noses in their mistakes, who do not look down on them as being teen-agers. But who can see them for the complexity which they are, have no need to institutionalize their weaknesses, nor fix in them the identity that they are to live as victims and patients of society.

"Ethical people open to joy" is one description of adults who are congruent with youth.

And the prevailing mood by which they tune in with youth culture is celebrative.

III.

Resources for Inventing

We begin now a series of chapters with which you might invent particular youth programs. Each chapter parallels the correspondingly numbered chapter in sections one and two of the book.

This series begins with some data that adult leaders of youth should do something about.

(1) A New Human Consciousness

We do have to deal with a new frame of consciousness.

A gap does exist between young people who have lived all their lives with electronic communications and entertainment world on the one hand, and adults and the church on the other. Particularly in the symbols they use, the way they make sense out of what happens, what communicates to them.

At two conferences in 1965 of adult youth leaders (total number, 320) the following items were frequently checked as "significantly true" on an instrument labeled "Frequent Weaknesses of My Communication as an Adult with Youth."

> 1. The "great words" my church uses in talking about the religious life have very little meaning for the youth of our community; they don't stir up anything real in them. Youth don't use them in thinking about their life, in making decisions, or dreaming futures.

133

2. Youth feels, thinks, decides, images, with a language different from the one I talk. And dreams about the future with imagery different from mine.

3. I don't know the words which a young person today uses in feeling, thinking, deciding, imagining.

4. I'm not "in." *I don't really understand the present youth culture* in my community. Or what's going on and where. It's an almost foreign world to me.

5. I'm predominantly seen as representing "the establishment," the *overhead* bureaucracy, the "expert" trying to take over, set tasks.

6. I don't do a very good job helping them develop their ideas.

7. I don't take enough care to be sure that I really understand all that the other person is saying. I often take off on a mistaken or surface idea of what he is saying.

8. I try to inform or advise or correct or convince instead of create with them.

9. We don't get down to *working through* their experiences. Everything stays external—not having to do with them. We just exchange opinions, and *never talk toward a decision* about anything.

10. I have great difficulty in getting the discussion down to where we are really living, deeply care about something, risk right then and there.

11. There is no communication of energy. I don't awaken youth. Nothing happens.

12. I'm tied too much to *exclusively verbal* communication. Too little *experiencing* together.

13. I give out conflicting signals. My tone of voice, relationship, attitudes are not in harmony with my words and announced intention. My verbal communication plays a different tune than my nonverbal communication.

Here are blocks to intersubjectivity between adults and contemporary young people. Also clues to where adult leaders must

134

improve their power to communicate with young people—to the degree they can.

The people checking these items were professional and semi-professional, not just random adults. More than many people of their communities, they had intermingled with young people. Yet they saw in themselves these inabilities to touch and engage in dialogue with young people. Is there a gap between two *eras of consciousness?*

If the "perceived leaders and guarantors" set the style and climate of any group as much as Kurt Lewin thought they do, then the communication strength and weaknesses of the central figures and the guarantors of a youth culture would determine the amount and quality of intersubjectivity which binds the group into one body. Specific training in communication needed by adult workers with youth could be set up.

(2) The Lived Moment as the Basis of Growth

At a conference of church youth workers in Kansas City, as a way of making progress on the importance of developing with young people a program of "perceiving, experiencing, sensing," of getting in touch with significant environment, we broke into groups of two for conversation on "One time recently in my life when I perceived and felt deeply, clearly, intensely, truly." With directions to make the story a three-stage journey.

> First—Describe the experience as vividly and fully as possible to the other person.
>
> Second—Describe some person who symbolizes for you this kind of life.
>
> Third—How important is it to have such experience of seeing clearly, feeling deeply, truly experiencing?

Here is an excerpt from one of the dialogues.

A: Actually, the experience that has meant the most to me ' recently was a trip that the Parish Ministry class at our seminary took to our state prison for men. A group of us went up there to examine the ministry to prisoners.

B: To find out what was being done for them?

A: We had that in mind. We were actually given the normal tour that anybody would be given, but over and and above that, we were allowed to sit down with five convicts. (And this is the term they prefer, convicts . . .)

B: Each of you personally, or the whole class?

A: The whole class sat down, and these five men were sitting in front of us, but in a way that separated us into twos. And then we were able to have dialogue, one with the other, each trying to understand what makes the other tick.

B: They were trying to understand what made you tick?

A: I truly believe they tried to understand what made us tick.

B: But how did this get started, so that they did this?

A: Well, they have the Seven Steps Program there, and each one of the men we talked with is a member of the committee of the Seven Steps Program. So they are already rather articulate about themselves. They're not shy or retiring people.

B: But the thing that made it good was that you weren't just examining them, but they were trying to understand you, too.

A: Yes, and so what stands out in my mind is a discovery. I had always believed the characteristic stereotype of a convict—that here is a man who is a rough, tough cookie, that you don't dare turn your back on. Here, at least two of these men were up for life, for murder. One had murdered a police officer in the act of robbery, and the other one had at least one murder that I know of, and he had already escaped twice from the prison. He was a known trouble-maker in the compound. When

137

the Seven Steps Program started, he came into this program with an antagonistic attitude, and his attitude has completely changed. Here were five men, each was different, but *each I could see as a true human being.* And I had never thought of a criminal as a true human being before. To be sure, loaded with problems—as I am loaded with problems. In the dialogue, I think that they were able to see that we have our own problems. But I know that every one of us that was there saw for the first time that they were true people with problems.

B: Let me press into this experience. Do you feel that in some ways you did become manifest to them, that you were able to be as open with them as they were with you?

A: Possibly not, in the group; but as a result of this visit, I made a trip back, and I visited the Seven Steps Program and their group therapy. And during this I spoke to two different prisoners. They weren't long conversations, and they weren't very deep conversations, but they implied, at least for me, that I was trying to become interested in them and to let them know that there was at least one person outside of the walls of that prison who knew they were there, and that they existed.

B: From this experience you carry in your mind a picture of these two meetings, rather than of just one person.

A: I think it would be the meeting rather than one person, although ... there is one man ...

B: One man who stands out?

A: The one man who stands out is the man who is the chairman of the committee. Here was a man who has led nothing but a life of crime, and now I saw him take that group of men in their own personal dialogue, and I could see him—as men were trying to hedge and to cut off their feelings—point them in a direction by saying, "Stop! Look at yourself and see if you're telling the truth about yourself. We all here are your friends. We may not like what you're saying, and we may not agree with you, but at least we're going to listen to you." As

I looked at this, I wondered, "Could I do this? Would I be willing to be honest enough to do what he was doing?"

B: This was a rather tremendous *experience,* not merely a seeing something. You began to experience that people can be transformed if there is somebody present to keep insisting and helping them be honest in their feelings and perceptions, and not try to play games with the group.

A: Yes, I think that's very true, and that's one of the first rules of the Seven Steps Program, being honest with yourself.

B: And there's in you now the tremendous surge that comes when a man changes his perception of other human beings.

A: I think that's true. Here I saw a man who had lived, I saw five men who just flat said, "All we know is crime. But now we see that those who we thought were fools or idiots were not so dumb; that we were the fools. And although we still to this day may not agree with everything that society says, and feel there's a lot of it that is wrong, we are in society, and we have to live by the rules of society or become mere animals."

B: What would have happened to you if you read a book about this movement—as contrasted to what actually happened to you when you encountered these people face to face? Is there a *big* difference?

A: Yes, very much so. If I had just read the book that has just come out, great as that book is, I don't think I would have become interested in these people ...

B: There is something to this idea that new perceptual experiences may be the real guts of learning.

A: Most definitely. If we don't experience something, if it's only an intellectual exercise, we really haven't learned. As a result of this, I will be going back this summer. I hope to spend as many Monday nights as I can with these men.

B: A future has opened up to you because of a *perceiving.*

It isn't just that the experience is good in itself, but a whole future opened here for you.

A: It's opened up a whole new area of possibility, and the whole experience opens up into related areas. Although I've been trained in psychology, it has made even that more meaningful. Because now I can see that if the hardened criminal is a person who has problems, this means that there is no person, no matter how detestable to me, who is not a person.

(3) Corporate Humanness

We have to be about establishing core moralities—ethical spine—if we would build culture for New Humanity. And keep man a bit human rather than a "barbaric." So what do we begin with?

Many people today are talking foolishly. As if they want an amoral world. As if there could be civilization *without* inner-directed men of lively conscience. And *with* a total lack of societal expectations and norms. They seem to think they would thrive in anarchy, and on the basis of an individual ethic.

There must be core moralities if there is to be a society anyone would care to live in, or if any life wants to take on distinctive shape and integrity. There has to be conscience if an appeal for justice is to bring a response from citizens. And without vigorous content, conscience is merely a faint bleat. A democratic society can survive only if large numbers of its citizens have inner controls.

The following is a beginning effort to identify what might go into the growth of contemporary ethical spine. To describe the paradigms of a healthy world.

We find core moralities partly by asking, "What goes into the making of a free and significant person?"

For morality is not commands and laws added on to life, but an actualizing of what man was meant to be. Morality is the path along which mankind can advance.

What is the mimimal core of morality absolutely necessary to realize personal life and bring off productive civilization?

Man has never been so bombarded with alternative styles of life. The clash is worldwide, and can result in making all of us more honest and decisive.

The sensitive adolescent feels that all kinds of voices—parents, teachers, books, entertainment celebrities, public opinion engineers—are attempting every hour of the day to gain entrance into his consciousness and seduce him to their style of life. His peer group in school and community often becomes a somewhat-to-be-feared place where clusters of adolescents of various levels of morality put pressure upon all who are devoted to quality in life. It seems that everyone is trumpeting "the *new* morality"—but on the basis that whatever is labeled "new" is right, and woe upon the old-fashioned. But which way is *life?*

Adolescents need to be able to hold their own in talking over "why or why not" with their peers. Parents are often unable to present much evidence or thinking which would support the morality they try to require of adolescents. So often adults end by throwing up their hands or acting as rigid authoritarians! Both adolescents and parents need to be able to state their positions in ways *intellectually and imaginatively exciting.*

We can strengthen the resources of young people who are making the good try. And develop core moralities in some adult guarantors for youth—for example, as an essential part of the training of public school teachers. Why not consider in high school and college the heart of the humanities—*life* philosophy? Rather than—as at present—doing it without benefit of ethical or religious disciplines but by exegeting the most irresponsible writings of alienated and disintegrated contemporary authors? What is needed is *adequate consideration of the nature of* personal *existence, the ends for which man lives, the meanings which the best men of all times and places have wrested out of life.*

So here is a beginning of ethical core. That we will never come to the same statement is not defeat. It is important that we all start thinking and deciding, and find areas of agreement.

For each morality we need to ask, "What experiences, events, persons, does this connect with? What fresh possibility does it offer? What could I add to its definition?"

Now for the first morality.

Movement Toward Authenticity

"Authentic or phony" is the basis on which our better young people divide adults into sheep and goats. They hope for themselves to be a truth, but are often knowledgeably doubtful.

Students have a violent distaste for the professor or student who pretends to be and believe what he is not. High school students detest people who are always "putting on an act"—particularly as they so often find themselves caught in such actions. The appeal of much literature is its cry, "Disengage yourself from the phoniness of adult society and conforming youth culture. Stay away from it as from the plague." Leading students of a seminary "came secretly by night" to congratulate a fellow student who had spoken to an ordaining committee what he really believed instead of what he was expected to say—at the cost of a year's deferment toward becoming a minister. In our better moments all of us feel nauseated when we are pressured into becoming "organization men," when we blur ourselves into whatever seems most powerful in our environment, when our

143

words and our actions go in different directions. In brief, we feel better when we are real.

What we're after is the morality of *striving for authenticity*.

Notice that the phrase is "*striving* for authenticity." Young people do not demand perfection of themselves or adults, but only that people be making the good try. That, in some dependable measure, they are what they *seem to be in public*. That they are in *movement toward* being authentic. The critical issue is—am I a *becoming* truth?

Young people today have a justifiable suspicion that adult society is like the cross-eyed cat who always had two saucers of milk before her—one to look at while she ate out of the other. They suspect that being an adult partly means looking at one "bowl" of morality while becoming "a fat cat" from a supply of a different morality. And being sort of relaxed about the fact that young people have to suffer the consequences of such immorality.

Young people also need some form of Geiger counter when they are around their own age group. What girl today can distinguish between "a line" and a real caring and respect for her? It is increasingly difficult for young people to know if their "love" for another is the real article or only the thin whine of pseudo-love on a short-playing platter.

Authenticity is more than just being open and psychologically honest—communicating what one really thinks and feels, acting out one's impulses.

Being authentic is being *the real article—Man.* (So we have to have some clues as to *what is* a *human* being.) It is becoming *a personal truth,* rather than merely learning about a lot of ideas that are true. (But being real does require ideas to back up one's convictions. A stupid clod is not authentic.)

A memorable image of authenticity might be—

Resonating with crystal clear tone—for the moment freed of impurities, blurred and confused existence. Communi-

144

cating the honest feeling from deep down, saying "yes" to the conviction struggling to be born. Being real *and* present.

Striving for being authentic is being a good friend of the *potential-to-be-person* that is packed within us. What is that potential? As understood by our religious heritage it is—

A desire to be manifest, and not to remain hidden
in this world
A wisdom that interprets what happens
A love that makes life subject-subject
A troth that even suffering cannot turn back.

"Being For"

Again and again the stark question hits us today: *Am I an agent of something significant*—or just taking it on the chin from a mediocre and impersonal world?

We can be tenacious in the face of adversity only if we believe the former of these alternatives. We need the morality of "being for."

Negro parents raise their children to live in a world where often they will be a minority that has to handle unusually difficult situations. Among other things, some have said to their adolescent sons and daughters: "This is America, and you can't allow other citizens to violate what America is. Nor to violate you as a human dignity and black man as an original source of new values."

For we are personally flabby unless our muscles are tendoned onto a cause or a people—something significantly greater than ourselves.

Healing for a person in distress begins with the discovery of commitment—some point at which the individual cares, feels responsible for something happening. It is not unwise repression that has led society to judge that commitment to a life enterprise

145

with one marriage partner awakens greater depths of love in mankind than episodically playing whoever is available in the field. And the businessman who is bringing off an enterprise is the one who finds life meaningful, rather than the "fast buck" fellow.

The "moaners and groaners" finally become sick of themselves. Man is a *time-consciousness*—a groping towards bringing off a future-past-present that is *"now* and in this particular here." To *be,* to project something, to live as responsible for the life or death of something—and not merely to have information and view life from a balcony—is our nature. To ask "What am I trying to bring off?" rather than "What past or external force caused me to do this?" is the road to health. "To what am I true?" is the great question for maturing ourselves. And therefore should not be too quickly or too easily answered.

Without a sense of vocation—of being called to do well some needed project in a particular time and place and with particular people—suffering is deadening and existence alien.

Commitment is being "for." And troth is the structure of life and the initiator of aliveness—even though it makes life tough at times.

Inevitably life puts us to facing—

What authority do I recognize other than "I want"?
Whom do I serve other than myself?
Where are the resources out of which I live?
What am I *for* in this present situation? What future
 am I helping bring off?
To what dare I be true over a stretch of time?

That these are nonsense questions to many people is a measure of our sickness as a civilization.

But what unspoiled adolescent wants to be forever unattached? Or forever a playbody? Only a victim and a sick patient?

146

Cocreating as Core Morality

Cocreating is the most mature form of love. Love is not just liking somebody.

The whole world is here—given to us. But we build our own little world in cooperation with the givens. We build co-personal worlds—i.e., worlds of which other people are a part.

1.

Insofar as these other people have helped to create this world, they are present as persons rather than as things. They are strugggling wills that have to be understood and taken account of as *agents*, not just as objects to be diagnosed and judged. We live *with*, rather than *alongside* (as we do with objects useful to us). Together we have structured a world of action, thought, feeling within which we collaborate. We are conjoint, communicated experience.

In a commercialized civilization, we tend to treat persons as faceless, as doing something useful for us, as powers to whom we must sell ourselves and our product. Yet there is a terrible hunger within us to be received as *person* and to love others in cocreation. "Living with" is both most violated and most desired by contemporary man.

2.

Establishing co-personal worlds is much more than just having pleasant human relations. It is designing and creating a somewhat endurable constellation of persons. Joint building of a little civilization—not just being amiable to all and sundry.

No world involving persons can be designed or sustained without communication. Or, more specifically, without communication that can be trusted. Much of public morality consists in letting others meet what we really think and feel, rather than in

147

passing by or lying to each other. Much of morality is honest communication. And healing its corruptions. So much so that we could well make communication a core morality all on its own importance. To choose life, we have to choose communication. And honesty of communication is a touchstone of one's integrity.

We can collaborate only with persons whom we understand, whose thoughts and feelings and intentions we have entered into.

By understanding and interiorizing others, we begin to establish for us that indispensable circle of people who regard each other as human beings. And begin to find our way in the evolutionary thrust toward a world net of thoughtful men who care about each other and know each other.

3.

A co-personal world—as contrasted with merely having pleasant times together—requires creative fidelity to those in that world.

The delinquent gang is often clearer on this point of faithfulness as the basic morality than the school club or church youth group. With them, if a person is not willing to suffer to the blood for the brethren and the purposes of the group, he is a coward and fit only for the outer darkness. The weakness in the fidelity of the usual gang is that it is not *creative* fidelity, but rather freezes its members at a level of premature and spurious adulthood.

Creative fidelity is a good definition of parenthood. Baffled, frustrated, eroded, feeling that their sons and daughters are too forcibly and prematurely weaning them as parents, today's adults are often not very good sources of the creative fidelity which full parenthood is. And this deficiency is inopportune for the adolescent.

To be a parent means to be a faithful friend of the growing which a son or daughter must do—come hell or high water.

Justice

Justice is the third core morality. "Where will I stand and fight for others? How do I overcome the evil I meet? In what ways do I support a *system* of justice?"

1.

Justice—on the inside of us—is our willingness to become involved when some other person's right to life and growth is being violated. To fight only when our own existence is constricted or threatened is not yet justice morality.

Back of this willingness to stand with others against the oppressor is a feeling, "We are all in this together; we are members one of another. And when fundamental rights are denied to any person, by just so much are the structures of human dignity and inclusiveness weakened for all of us."

2.

Justice—objectively—is these structures of human dignity and inclusiveness. Justice is laws—and power to enforce them—that apply to everyone. It is democratic institutions rather than governance by personal whim, brute force, or a power elite. Justice is the rules of the game which we mutually enforce, the recognition that an opponent has a right to be heard.

Justice is more than fighting against injustice. It is also institutions and customs which positively *invite and nurture the human potential* of people. Justice includes the opportunity to know, to grow, and to develop one's potential.

Justice is not just an individual issue; it is a communal matter. It is also a larger co-personal world than our world of intimate acquaintance. Not all things can be solved on a face-to-face individual basis. For instance, a community ought to have the power to defend its children and youth against brutalizing and pornographic literature, sadistic and sex-obsessed movies and television. For if the local community is rendered powerless—or its fight for its children and youth becomes too involved and never decisive—the community's sense of itself as "We are *able*" and its sense of being responsible, disintegrate. And then our civilization's culture is determined only by the license of the fast-buck boys who use children and youth for exploitative purposes.

3.

There is no better tradition in which man might unite the world over than the prophetic cry—

> Let justice roll down as waters
> And righteousness as a mighty stream.

For decades we have depended upon sports to inculcate in adolescents a sense of fair play and treating an opponent with respect. This probably no longer comes out of present-day athletics in high schools and colleges. The present pressure upon coaches to win or lose their jobs, the guffaws of worldly wise skepticism among athletes when fair play and sportsmanship are mentioned in connection with sports, the violent aggression by spectators at and after games buttress the recent radical conclusion that we will have to search for some other institution in which justice can be learned by participation. In America the learning arena is probably the struggle for black man and white man to relate to each other as equal powers.

Idea Power

In a very complex world, basic morality must include the effective will to be intelligent. To own ideas whose time has come. Life continues to have excitement and power only to those who have ideas. Who have come to enjoy the stirring of the mind.

For whom to enter into the great experiences and meanings of life gained by the forefathers is not an assignment, but a self-sustained project. And because it greatens their humanity, not because it will get them a higher salary.

Another name for intelligence is Wisdom. Wisdom in man is knowing—experientially—the structures by which life was, and continues to be, created. Wisdom is living out of meanings, rather than mere fact or sensations. Wisdom is a tested awareness of "What is struggling to be born in this moment of history? In me? When I am actualizing what man was meant to be? What am I?"

To know some one thing in depth is part of the morality of being intelligent. It adds to our integrity. We better know who we are when we can identify ourselves with some field of knowledge and expertness. We can respect ourselves.

Who can live wholeheartedly without some sense of what is real and some fairly precise ideas of what the real is?

The morality of being intelligent is possible only when it is settled public policy that all citizens have access to necessary information. Each citizen must require of himself some tendency to think in terms of long-range direction, some honesty in labeling matters for what they are rather than using morally high-sounding titles. The inhabitants of today's world need to be able to distinguish between life and death in the ceaseless flow of happenings as reported in the news.

This kind of society may resist the photogenic personality, the golden voice of pseudo-destiny, the terrorizers. Striving to be intelligent is a minimal morality for a society blessed and cursed with mass communications, where possession of the air waves is by advertisers and propagandists.

We live in a time when a new world consciousness is being created. We also are immersed in what has been called "menticide," the destruction of what makes mind possible: a) the murdering of words so that they no longer mean; b) the paralyzing of each person's *personal* identity; c) the establishing of identification with the brutal, the intense desire to live in solidarity with mankind's enemies; d) the grooving of the long-playing record, which keeps on playing in young people's consciousness without any correction by apprenticeship to the real.

Who *offers* young people an invitation to think, to create fresh ideas which will stir their generation's making of history?

Being Freedom

"To do as one pleases" is the simple definition many have of freedom. But it is important to realize that freedom is not just one thing. *Many* conditions of our self-in-the-world are bound together to form the grandeur of freedom.

1.

Freedom is *spontaneity* utterly absorbed in doing fairly well something which expresses personal truth. In such moments, we are living the expressive, rather than the reactive and dependent life. The suckling is not free.

Such freedom exists only with competency—only when our powers are disciplined and interfused with enabling ideas and craftsmanship. Freedom is "I am able to." To hold my own in encounter, to incarnate the dream stirring in my imagination. To improvise well, express in significant form the feeling and existence stirring in me. If I do not possess this freedom because I do not have the necessary skills, I am unfree.

To be free is to be able to exert power—so that we share in the self-determining done by our group, community, nation. Freedom is participating in building worlds.

Courage is a built-in part of freedom's spontaneity. For to express one's considered truth means to stand out with some distinctiveness from the social blur, and become vulnerable to being shot down.

2.

Freedom is also the absence of raw restraint and compulsion put upon us by an environment determined to condition us and to do the planning of life for us. Or, if not the absence of such restraints, our partially successful rebellion and resistance to such external pressures. Since we live in a world that does not leave us alone, freedom is the strength and inner toughness that enables us successfully to resist being torn to pieces, our center of decision obliterated, the boundaries of our selfhood diffused.

3.

Personal freedom begins for us at the moment we take responsibility for our behavior. For it is thus that we cease to be children or mass man governed by something outside ourselves. Taking responsibility, being held responsible for the consequences of our choices and actions, is the birth of our powers of self-regulation.

But this does not automatically guarantee freedom, for our inner world may be so driven and possessed by hostilities, estrangements, self-despising, split-off appetites, that we repeat impulse and memories rather than express spontaneity.

4.

Our freedom is also our power to imagine new things which are not yet, and toward which we can live. We need not be hopelessly trapped in what already is. A human being lives much of the time in expectancy and toward some future which he sees and desires. Anytime he finds his life reduced to "imageless deeds," he feels depersonalized.

Human beings live in *meanings*, rather than biological events. And living in meanings, they have more maneuverability to their lives, for they need not stick so closely to particular

153

habitual behaviors. The *human* being can delay and improve his responses. Between the stimulus which the world hurls at him and his responding action, he can interpose some thinking, imagining, exploring a range of live options.

5.

And finally, freedom is to be a functioning part of some network of relationships. To be confirmed and respected by an organized group of "others." To have demands made upon us by these people which awaken development within us, and yet allow us some privacy. Man is depersonalized unless he has communication and communion stretching out to and from him into the world. To be surrounded by impervious people is unfreedom. To be impervious ourselves is to be shut up, a captive in bondage,

"Eyeless in Gaza at the wheel with slaves."

Person—Perception

All relationships begin with perception. So do all our actions.

"In our time, young people—and just *people* are breaking out all over the world to know people in other countries. To understand what they make of life, what makes them tick, what can be expected of them.

"There is future for one who is skilled in person-perception. Who can tune into the inwardness of another person, catch understandingly his identity of that moment." [1]

For most of us, persons are the most interesting thing in the whole world. They are sources of best insight into how it feels to be a person and what the possibilities of human life are. We could become powerfully human if we could but perceive enough of them correctly.

[1] Ross Snyder, *On Becoming Human* (Nashville: Abingdon Press, 1967), pp. 43-44.

154

Many people we do not want to see correctly. Always we tend to see a person with the help and hindrance of our life project as of the moment. We almost always partly distort, and certainly always very incompletely grasp, what is going on for them.

Nor do we want to be seen correctly by them. They are not the kind of people we want to know us. Or we are scared we would be rejected and hurt by them if they saw us as we really are. So we run to hide so we won't be seen, we expose only our surfaces, we camouflage, we lie. And the other person is doing the same. No wonder the battle of images—(1) my image of myself, (2) the other's image of me, (3) my perception of what he sees in me and the attitude he takes toward it, (4) his perception of what I see in him—so often is divisive.

While I'm sizing him up as I act, he's sizing me up at the same time. And revealing that of himself which he wants me to see, perhaps what he thinks I want to see. I probably am condemned to seeing only what he wants me to see. But is it *him?* So I am never sure whether I'm perceiving a person accurately or not. Always I must keep saying, "There is more to him than I see."

So it would be entirely appropriate to begin the confession of sin in the morning church services of this country with a confession of the immoralities of our person-perceptions of that week.

Much of the sinning of the white man toward the black lies in his *habits of seeing.* At least, distorted seeing and lack of seeing is one important source of his imperviousness. We might make progress if white men would begin to explore their method of perceiving other people. And take skill training in person-perception. The need is mutual.

"You shall perceive other people accurately" could well be a phrase used so often in our inner speech to ourselves that it becomes an active part of our conscience. Particularly by every leader of the human enterprise.

Summary

We and world civilization need to find a minimal core of moral existence which we are willing to be.

Seven core moralities are peculiarly relevant for young people today. And for adults.

Striving for authenticity
Being "for"
Cocreating and communicating
Justice
Idea power
Being freedom
Person-perception

These moralities are what man is when he is actualizing himself as person. They are potential—but not guaranteed. With these he can take responsibility for his life. He can *be*.

But they cannot be merely *individual*. They must also be the paradigm structures of a civilization. We have a *culture* only when there are dependable communal structures of existence.

Life is not just a struggle for more and better cars and unceasing entertainment. Nor is America. Life is an arena for the achievement of moral man and a world net of thoughtful men in honest communication with each other.

Everywhere, everyone seeks a focus which will give form, purpose, order, significance to his life—and to the common life. From where is this focus to come? What goes into the making of a free and significant person? And culture?

How do you regard the seven proposed moralities? What would you propose?

(4) People with Whom You Can Make Yourself

Along what lines could young people develop the interpersonal?

Relational Ministries

There are five relational ministerings going on in an indigenous Christian culture—the ministries of authenticity, of personal revelation, of understanding, of the great conversation, of culture content.

These ministerings are the functionings by which we build "our colony." Training in them would be important.

The program of any center of world life would include both experiencing and some teaching about them, so these "goings on" might be understood and purposed. Members' abilities to perform these ministries would be developed into competency.

1. The Ministry of Authenticity

The structure of the responsible life includes a mutual ministry to help each other center down and live out of *fundamental truths.*

This could be described as helping people to become the Single One. Not so much in Kierkegaard's sense, but in Buber's meaning of the word—that one must be able to meet each fresh situation with a spontaneous wholeness, responding out of the depths of his nature rather than in terms of previously decided rules or images.

In the youth enterprise of the future, we will have more opportunity for "retreats" of weekends or a week, and more competence in conducting them. Young people need occasions where they may cut off the rush and pressure of life as it must be lived and the triviality in which it often is lived, and center down for an uninterrupted period of time to consider such down to earth questions as "My style of relating to people," "Who am I when I'm most alive?" "What objects and events tell me the kind of person I really am?" "A truth I particularly hope my life puts into the world," "To what am I true?" "When have I met tremendous mystery, transcendence?" "Communication or prattle? Encounter or evasion?" "What story of life enables me to make sense out of what happens to me?"

Erich Fromm believed a certain malady characterized American civilization—we all tend too much to become the "marketing personality," trying very hard to sell ourselves to others, rather than being authentically an integrity that is a truth. In such a society, communal cultivation of the ethos of authentic existence would help an exodus from this Egypt.

Perhaps our greatest ministry to inner-personal events in another is to be an integrity ourselves. To be a personal integrity that has found what he is true to and what is true to him, that encounters rather than evades or conforms, that stands out in some clearness of structure rather than hides or dissolves, that must be taken account of, that can be dialogued and cocreated with, with whom others can know where they stand. Whenever such a person is met, a welcome sanity and undizziness is possible.

2. The Mutual Ministry of Self-Revelation

A man is not a man until he has stated his truth with vigor before a group and in a situation where it can be challenged, shaped, forced to come to terms with the boundaries of other people's views. We cannot be sure that we know him until he does.

To have the privilege of declaring oneself is an important opportunity of growth. For self-definition comes partly through trying to give form to our diffused experiences and feelings in such a way that they become clarified to others and ourselves. And take on order and design.

Yet how hidden most people remain; how little they take on the ministry to others (and themselves) of personal revelation—partly because they feel that they don't know enough to make a statement, partly because they have grown up in schools and in a society where somebody is always telling them what to think and what to buy. Also partly because when they have attempted to reveal themselves they have met with attack and defeat. So our churches and schools and community organizations are filled with members who remain opaque, who have never found a status and role which invites them to declare themselves.

So we never quite know who and what we are living with. To some degree we are always fearful of the others—and of trust. We sense there are hidden phantoms about us. Oh, that they would become manifest!

3. The Ministry of Understanding and Midwifery

There is no saving communion with others unless the personal revelation is received. When we come to know that the way we see and feel things can be significantly seen and felt by another human being, we are joined to the human race. Anxiety and estrangement for the time being are nonexistent. Only as we become aware that another person understands *us* (and not just our ideas) are we released to be ourselves.

Understanding is the relationship which creates, heals, and fulfills.

A fully Christian group would be a place where there are people who have trained capacity for the understanding that releases those they meet from locked-up strangeness, unglues them from their fears and hatreds, enables them to flower into fresh life.

The process of midwifery is a part of the ministry of understanding.

Midwifery is not declaring to others *our* truths. It is rather a ministry of helping bring to birth the thought, feeling, new creation that is a faint stirring within the other. This stirring requires a certain kind of human relationship if it is ever to see the light of day and become a lusty infant running around in our common life. For the new and yet unexpressed thought, feeling, transformation of character is always a very fragile thing. Too quick and vigorous criticism or defeat may destroy it utterly.

It needs an encouraging climate and a soil in which to grow. The emerging new life needs to feel welcome in our world so that it may have the courage to assume distinct form and grow into maturity.

It requires both artistry and religion to meet people in the context of creation. To let the new that is struggling to be born within them take the lead and to follow it, rather than trying to take over their development within our own hands and impose upon it the shape and direction of what we already are. To act as midwife to the religious impulses of those about us.

4. The Ministry of the Great Conversation

The Great Conversation is the play of mind with mind upon the things that matter most in life.

160

The Great Conversation is a small group of people matching themselves against the great problems of life that have to be decided in *their* existence. The assumption is that more will be awakened within all by the honest bringing in of experiences from many people, and by the impact of mind upon mind. Decision may not be immediately pressed for. Those present are not just talking about what they will do tomorrow, but getting more penetrating insight into the depth of the situation in which they live, and catching its hovering significance.

At its best, the Great Conversation has unexpected surprises, the flash of imagination, the togetherness of everyone joined in the chase of "a rabbit" that has been flushed out of a thicket of human experience. Since the group is trying for the truth, it is a cooperative game, not a debate. Neither is it meandering conversation. It is not some people trying to impress other people by remarks about the latest play, or by unloading lecturettes upon them. While it is not primarily judgmental conversation, fuzziness of thought or actual fraud is not allowed to go unchallenged. So it is intellectually "sharp." It is a leaping fire that awakens fire within each.

The mind reports a feeling of zest; it is felt as an experience of the life of the mind at its best. Participation in such conversation is an intense form of fun.

The conversation is great because of both its quality and its content. In quality, it is two-way communication and I-Thou relationship in intellectual pursuit. In content, it is a conversation about living life greatly, rather than in mediocre fashion, and so about emerging ideas and issues felt to be significant.

There is all too little opportunity for such conversation. Many people have gone through college and adult life without ever being a part of such. But without such conversation, good thinking about the existentials of life will not go on within individuals. For it is not just in hearing a good mind think out loud that our mind grows. We awaken and grow the powers of our mind by trying to express and communicate what we think to other people.

Not only does the fulfillment of personal life require participation in the great conversation. There is no other good way of building up the mind of a society, a cohesive team, an indigenous culture. That so many people and groups today have no mind is partly because of lack of this communication of ideas and experiences about things that matter most.

Further, without this Great Conversation the various members will not know what each other thinks and feels, or where other members will take a stand and not run. Therefore, all are afraid to take a courageous stand, lest they be left out all alone. Members split in all directions on issues and are unable to exist as a power in the life of society.

Some of this conversation will be in groups of five to twelve people, some will be of only two people.

Good conversation is a major factor in education. Why should only people in trouble have the privilege of intimate conversation with teachers, pastors, other significant adults? We need the Great Conversation to nurture the depth, the feeling and idea power of young people who are making the good try and will be leaders of the enterprises of civilization.

5. Dialoguing with Culture Content

Many young people in our times are not so much mean as their minds and emotions are empty; not so much too strong and prideful as so empty and thin that they cannot stand. One of the important ministries today is the ministry of "talking with" resources of culture.

"Culture" does not mean art or a surface graciousness. Culture is the great images by which persons live, the recurring experiences which organize personal life and civilization, the great memories of individual and historical events where the meaning of life broke through, the wealth of feeling and purposing out of which creative powers are again and again called forth. Culture is therefore more than mere information or *knowledge about* religion and history.

Such content of culture must be made available to young people in such a way that they can appropriate it. Otherwise they will live with the thinness of guiding images, experiences, meanings, and feelings that come from their own little range of experience. Condemned to living just with their own, ultimately they reach out to some demonic form to fill the emptiness within them and to secure social validation.

Culture content must be packaged in *personal form* if it is to be understood and received into our motivations. We must encounter goodness and truth in living flesh. A measure of anyone's maturity as person is therefore not what he knows, but the persons he knows in depth.

Therefore the ministry of culture content is not primarily the usual kind of education at all, but rather training ourselves and others in the art of "entering into"—the art of entering into the inner world of the people of all times and places (including our own) who have lived life with *peculiar intensity and integrity.*

This means not approaching these lives so much from the standpoint of analyzing them and spreading the parts out in patterns of logic, but approaching their lived moments and inner world appreciatively—interiorizing them, taking them into ourselves as a whole, trying to acquire awareness of how these persons encountered life and the struggles deep within them for their own authenticity. Meeting such a man arouses us, not to imitate him but to discover and express our own integrity.

This is not the usual laudatory treatment of a man's life and then an urging that we do certain things. It is a centered effort to acquire the inner world of other men and the hidden significance of crucial events.

Fellowship is not merely liking each other, but common possession of significant culture!

MINISTRY IN THE SOCIAL STRUCTURE SYSTEM
OF THE PUBLIC SCHOOL

There are social structures in all junior and senior high school groups. And if young people are to build a youth culture fit for human beings, this is an important place of action. Further, it is vitally important that any youth leader know exactly in what order each individual in his community is listed by those who go to school with him.

Almost every junior high school society has a very rigidly structured group system in which number one, two, and three are easily identified and identifiable. The problem seems to be that most adults are afraid to approach this structure; therefore, most teen-agers believe that the structure is more important than anything else since adults cannot seem to control it. It would seem most important for teachers and school systems to deal with this problem before any other single educational problem. Once this is dealt with and the teen-agers feel that there are adults who do have some insight and control into the situation in which *they* live, the interpersonal relationships may begin to take place because the blocks are then removed.

Not until these blocks are removed can interpersonal relationships begin to move through the group, because up until this time the leaders of the group will be too fearful to allow much freedom of movement. Once a high school girl gave us detailed information about how she completely controlled her entire school class from the fourth grade through the eighth grade. She tells how she managed to intimidate the entire group so that no one would make a move without first consulting her. She tells us how at the end of the sixth grade year she realized that boys were going to be an important factor in the female social structure within the next few years, and she began to line up the boys so that she had control over who liked whom and which boys would come to the parties. She found it very important to be in absolute control of the boy-girl dating party structure.

These things too often go unnoticed by the adult and teaching communities. Too often teen-agers who are very much desirous of becoming a self cannot do so because other teen-agers are too destructive. They do not wish to be destructive; they know no other way without some adult entering in to help them.

We need more talk about how we stop going to war with one another in the local school where we ignore one another. And about how we integrate our own society in which the status people tend to ignore those who have no status and vice versa. In other words, the school systems and adults must begin to deal with the real war and the real struggle to participate which is going on right under their very noses in the communities in which they live. Too often talking about things which are far away is only an excuse to blow out those frustrations which the young people are actually experiencing in their own community now. It then becomes another way to avoid acting, and we become caught in the trap of *talking about* action.

This is to say that only in the midst of the world is Christ, Christ. And therefore we must talk about what is going on in the midst of *our* world, not in the midst of someone else's world eight thousand miles away. This is not to say that we should ignore other worlds, but to say that we must first deal with our own world. For Bonhoeffer, the world is the nearest Thou. Therefore, that group of people must be dealt with now. One of our high school leaders has suggested that we gather together the young men of the high school community to discuss what kind of girls they would like to date and that they, therefore, influence the kinds of girls which develop in the local high school community.[1]

[1] Contributed by Gabe L. Campbell, Minister of Youth, Second Congregational Church, Greenwich, Connecticut.

THE COFFEEHOUSE

In the coffeehouse ministry, teens work with supportive adults in determining all things. Secondly, the coffeehouse is a place where everyone is accepted as he is. Differing opinions are exchanged without fragmenting the relationships. Thirdly, the coffeehouse is a setting where significant adults participate with teens in the task of being human to each other.

The coffeehouse for teen-agers is a place where the theological process of becoming more fully human before God in the presence of a neighbor happens. Theology flows and becomes a style of life rather than the recital of predetermined dogma. Sitting at tables with others creates a communion between persons which encourages personal confrontation (confession), acceptance (forgiveness), giving (discipleship). The secular and sacred are interrelated. The coffeehouse is not the answer to all of youth's needs. However, it does reveal an important response to what the institution has failed to do.[2]

[2] Contributed by Dennis C. Benson, Director of Youth Ministry, Council of Churches of the Pittsburgh Area.

(5) Break-out and Celebration

What is communal celebration? Here is a series of images into which you can pour your own content.

    1. Celebration is a million candles lit with reverence and joy.

        God is exuberance; are we then to plod along unfilled by the intensity at the heart of things?

    2. Celebration is a crash of cymbals and a torrent of trumpets pouring through cracks in the drum roll of death and destruction.

        The rotted past and the disappearing present shall not have dominion!

    3. Celebration is sensing the incognito liturgy within the news events of the world of that day.

        Choose you this day whom you will serve.

    4. New time invades our consciousness.

        World-for-us begins its metamorphosis.

5. Celebration is the yeast of imagination transforming events into the daily bread of the soul.

> Amazement, shudder, ecstasy awaken. The kingdom of God becomes present in the lived moment.

6. Celebration is offering the creation and agony in this day to a transforming God.

> And new possibility appears.

7. Celebration is the journey of the stars seen through a telescope; the beating of heart muscle seen through an electron microscope.

> What's really working is revealed.

8. Celebration is the sudden rush of meaning that happens when things come together.

> Jumble and chaos fall into pattern. "Eureka! Allelulia!" We finally see ourselves in home territory, and we shout "Amen!"

9. Celebration is a certain way of singing "When I Survey the Wondrous Cross."

> With recognition and realization.

10. Celebration is entering into the creating and redeeming which is now making mankind. With a certain amount of reckless abandon.

> We are hilariously tuned into God and fellow man.

11. Celebration is a people sitting out through time toward a destiny, with a treasure of memories and expectancies.

> There is a song to be sung, a journey to be made, a territory to be colonized.

Guide to Constructing a Celebration

I. *What's going on in the world? So importantly that we should take account of it? Where do we stand in it?*

The liturgy of profane man . . . and the Christ liturgy . . . of this day in the world.

Placing ourselves where the action is . . . where history-making is going on . . . where—
  human dignity is expressing itself
  love of God and man is breaking out
  agony, despair, powerless, brutality . . . battle to overcome man
  new potential in this moment of history-making can be sensed.
How express these *strikingly*
  in sound, light, music, lived moment, lyric?

II. *What experiencing . . . what lived moment in which we are all caught up . . . do we have to celebrate?*

How enter into its depths and recesses? Feel it freshly. Retaste and relive, intensify and distill, wonder and joy in it. Celebrate the presence of new possibility—that a new beginning of our existence begins to burgeon. "This day a future is present."
  How move this experiencing into meaning . . . out of which we live and move and have our being?
    How "art" it so it comes through with its significance showing? In
      original soul music and lyric
      conversation by two people up front working the experience over
      skit, coffeehouse play, movie . . . that presents a hunk of experience still pulsing blood.

III. *Where is the cluster of people with whom we can make ourselves and a world? A body of persons moving the world.*

What is their enterprise? The making things happen which we want to be part of?

169

Their present decisive battle that has to be won?
What their life style is. A person who is vividly this life.
Their troth. How bonded and knit together—"members one
on another"? The immediacy possible with the Innermost
Moving.

IV. *Truth that needs to be put into the world*
    ...with everything we've got.

The *life world* we are bringing off, the idea whose time has
    come ...
The break-out into the world by our people that transforms
    some bit of world.
The common hope, zeal, expectancy, re-membering in the
    body of Christ, which is pulsing...
Put into memorable phrase and action.

A celebration is a way of creating culture
What can you create and offer to your generation?
    What
        sounds
            pulsing
                lyric and song
                    two-way dialogue
                        words speaking experiences
                            newscast and interpretation
                            dramatic vignettes
                                poems
                                    litanies
                                        art—visual liturgy
                                            banners, painting
                                                symbolic communal action
    would present what you can offer ...
        in *significant* form
        enabling the spontaneity of others to come out?

Celebration Is Not a Theater "Happening"

It is important to keep clear the difference between "happenings" and what we are talking about when we say "communal celebration."

All kinds of things go on under the name of "happenings." Sometimes what is meant is a free coming together and letting what will, emerge. Such openness would be an invitation to spontaneity and would be fun.

But a whole school of thought and invention, particularly in theater, of a quite different intent, is growing up. Its scheme is "multiple sensations"—and to some degree all of us today are committed to multilayered perceptions and meanings. But it is "against interpretation," and seemingly on the schizoid and psychotic side of life. It is an interesting new attempt in theater, but appears to have an entirely different attitude toward people and the mind of man than I find congenial.

The following points, suggested to my mind after reading *Happenings* by Michael Kirby, establish differences between a happening, and spontaneous art which comes out and is controlled by the propulsion of the people who are arting. These criteria make clear the difference between a happening and a *celebration,* as we are inventing it. As I see it, a happening (as defined in Kirby's book) is an apothesis of the sickness of technological society and stimulus-response behaviorism. Fortunately there seem to be some indications that happenings will break out of this beginning nature and definition.

What Constitutes a Happening?

1) *"Contrived environment"* surrounds and encloses "victim" on all sides

2) *Disintegrating the usual structures* of perception, of organizing the world verbally, of attitudes: "Oh I know what it is, I have my mind all made up already."

171

3) *Compartmented Structures and Happenings*
    Theatrical units—each part self-contained
        Simultaneous presentation of unrelated (logically) events
        A massive vibratory collage
4) *No public matrix of time, place, character*
5) *Performers in physical proximity* (maybe) but not of psyche. Their juxtaposition is only functional; they are not *personally* related, or in cocreation. The performers are a prop, part of the "thing" environment.
6) *Not a picture, but action painting. Sound painting.*
7) *No interpretation. Dissociation* and sensory qualities predominate.
    Programmed sensations.
    Diffused vision; no intentional arc developing;
        words often drawn at random.
    Pictures a hostile, cold world that doesn't even care enough
        to hate you.

(6) Process Lived Moments into Culture

Here are two illustrations of phenomenologizing by young people. Notice again the three steps.

They have each taken a lived moment, experienced and looked into its depth instead of just its surface happening. Raw experience has been processed into meaningful world and future self. Having been opened to the revelation which they and life were co-making, they now have more resources with which to live.

And they are beginning to master the habits and discipline of such achievement.

A LIVED MOMENT

a. Description

The sound of the roaring, pounding waves engulfed me, permeated me, caught me up in its dreadful, deadly

173

rhythm. As surely as I could not escape the sound of the waves, neither could I tear my eyes away from the foaming brown surf. A powerful fascination—a spell akin to hypnotism—held me in its windy grip. My hair blew in my eyes and mouth, and my white summer shirt flapped around me, affording little protection from the chill.

I was standing on a beach on the Texas coast, and Hurricane Beulah was only a few hundred miles away. In the early afternoon, my mother and I had driven the few miles from our home to see what the waves looked like, before it got too dangerous to come out. There were other people on other parts of the beach, but we had found a spot to ourselves. The wide sandy beach had disappeared, and only a small part of it could be seen when the ocean drew up into itself in preparation for another attack on the hard-packed sand road. The road that had once gone straight out onto the beach found today that the ocean had swallowed much of the soft sand from around it, leaving the harder sand of the road standing exposed two feet above the remaining beach. Bit by bit the ocean was claiming that also. As we stood there at the road's end and watched the water repeatedly advancing across the beach to lap at the road and then retreat, one after another, sections of the gravelly, hard-packed road would give way with a sigh and a thud. The next advance of the hungry water would reduce the broken piece of road to a smooth mound of sand and the next attack and retreat would swallow the mound of sand into itself.

All my senses were saturated by the sound which seemed to come from all around, by the sight and smell of the turbulent water, by the cold, excited wind. But it was not only my five senses that the moment possessed. My very spirit was caught up in the scene. My spirit caught the wind's excitement; the smell and the chill of the air I breathed filled me with elation; the sound wanted to draw me into it; the sight of the pounding waves and the sinister advance across the beach and the terrifying sucking back into itself frightened, yet fascinated me.

What I felt was a heightened form of the fascination waves always have for me. Nothing else in all nature fascinates me as waves do. I've watched them creep gently, softly across soft sand, and then sink back again with a whisper; I've watched more excited waves pound upon each other just offshore, sending a rolling rush of water tumbling across the sand. I cannot look at waves with the indifference that we usually look at grass and trees and sky, because for me the ocean is alive and personal. I feel as if it has a spirit, as if perhaps it would communicate with me.

Though I have felt that way before, never have I felt it with such intensity as on that day. The water seemed to have a passionate determination to devour everything on the beach. While we watched, it sucked a log into its watery body, and it beat relentlessly on the road at our feet. I felt as if it wanted me, and I could hardly hold myself where I stood. A strange, unexplainable feeling lured me toward the water, like a woman to a man, or perhaps the lemmings to the sea.

The feeling was to a great part the dare, the lure, of excitement and thrill. I wanted to play in the water the same way many others wanted to go into the water with their surfboards. I desired the physical thrill of swirling waters around me. I didn't really feel afraid of the water. Waves have rarely hurt me, and there's a thrill even to being knocked over or sucked under by a wave—as long as you are able to escape it and recover. I like to feel the strong water rushing around me, pushing me, carrying me. So I wanted this time to run into the waves like on any other day at the beach.

But today was different. I knew, not so much from natural knowledge as from acquired knowledge, that the water was dangerous. Within easy eyesight from where I stood, cars and men were gathered in a desperate, desolate, hopeless wait for the sea to give up the body of a sixteen-year-old girl who had dared the sea that morning with her surfboard.

Nothing made me feel more strongly that the sea was

175

alive and personal than that knowledge that she had taken that girl and that she held her out of the desperate reach of those people on the shore.

I was standing face to face with nature, as if I were looking her straight in the eyes and thereby into her very being—and I saw her strength, her perseverance, her ruthlessness. She was not malevolent—intending evil—but she was strong and unbending. And to be unbending is to be without mercy.

b. What Was the Existence?

I experienced that afternoon a vivid confrontation with the forces of nature. It was a moment of really *seeing* nature, not just taking it for granted. More than that it was seeing nature as a force, as being alive, as a "will" to be dealt with. In that moment, I "recognized" Nature as a being that is not man-made and man-controlled. She has her own ways, her own rules, her own tricks. She is not a respecter of persons—no man can command the sea to cease her rolling.

It was a moment in which the precariousness of life was impressed upon me. I was so close to the inviting water; I could easily have run into it as if to play, as I had so many times before, but this time . . . the undertow . . . Just up the beach from me, men paced back and forth across the sand where a girl had done just that—a girl whose body now was surely tossing around facedown somewhere out in the gulf, being beaten relentlessly by wave upon wave. Life could go that easily? We forget that most of the time. We accept our lives as given, as ours, as if it would be hard to die—harder certainly than stepping off the road and running into the sea to see what it feels like.

I saw man's weakness and transitoriness in contrast to the strength and enduringness of nature. A life had been snuffed out, but the sea pounded on uncaring. A family was in agony, but the world moved on unheeding.

c. Theologizing

When I behold the ocean's strength . . . what is man?

When man forgets his finiteness, his frailty, he is forgetting his true nature. He is proud and believes he has a claim on life. He believes the world owes him health and wealth and, most of all—life.

But man has no claim on his life. Through no virtue or accomplishment of his own, man is given life, and the thread of life is tenuous—easily broken. Because life is a gift, man is, in the very nature of his being, *indebted* to the Him who grants life. The giver of life has a claim on him to whom he gives life. Man, then, instead of having a claim on life, finds that life has a claim on him. Not owning his life—not being able to say when his life shall be finished can man say, "I shall live for myself now and pay my debt to God and man tomorrow"? Can he say, "This is *my* life to live as I desire"?

DATING

I maneuvered the car into a parking place in front of her house and switched off the motor and lights. For a good part of the evening I had been anticipating this moment. What would I do? How would she respond? Would I simply take her to the door and bid a polite "thank you and good night"? Would I tenderly embrace her? Would I passionately "make out" with her? Would I go to bed with her? How would she respond to me? What would she *let* me do? I was trembling all over, but not from the chill of the night. I wanted to possess her . . . hungered to touch her . . . to taste her lips . . . to crush her body to mine.

She was wearing an orange mini-skirt and black knit stockings, which well revealed her shapely legs. And she didn't keep tugging at her skirt each time she caught me glancing that way. That gave me some cause for encouragement.

We exchanged a few nervous, superficial remarks, and then I reached—lunged—pulling her into a passionate embrace. For the next few moments we exchanged innumerable brutal kisses. No words. She seemed as starved for affection—as lonely—as I.

With each new advance I was swept with waves of fear and guilt. A busy public street, in front of her home. What if her parents should look out the window? What if a neighbor should pass by?

Memories raced through my mind of other girls I had treated the same way—and some I had treated differently. Why? What had been different? Was Barbara any different from Julie?

Maybe the difference lay in what the individual meant to me—in what my hopes and expectations were for the relationship. I didn't care if I ever saw this girl again. Maybe I wouldn't even *want* to see her again. She was a "one nighter." Why did it matter if I hurt her? She'd get over it. After all, she must be enjoying it as much as I. Enjoying it? Was I really enjoying it? What does that mean? We don't love each other—at least I don't love her. Could she possibly love me? No . . . impossible. We only met this evening. We don't even know each other. What could she expect? What will be her expectations as a result of this? She must be lonely, must be husband-hunting. Well—it won't be me! This chick is too damn insecure! How can she let me do this to her? How can she expect me to respect her? But what about me? Am I any more secure? Should I expect any respect from her?

We passionately tumbled about the front seat for a while longer, and finally I suggested that it was late and perhaps I should take her in. Actually I was hoping that she would invite me in and that we might accidentally tumble onto a couch, a bed—anything but the front seat of a car.

We silently walked to the door. I mumbled something about enjoying the evening and that I would like to see her again—an obvious lie. She whispered a rather confused assent and silently disappeared.

What, as I later perceived it, were the realities of this "lived" moment?

I slowly walked toward my car, feeling very depressed and lonely. I was disappointed and angry with myself. The idea of authenticity clubbed me. Man, how phony can a guy be? Maybe Julie was insecure, but what had I done to affirm her sense of worth as a person? I had responded to her in a completely selfish and inhuman manner. I had considered her only as an object—a thing to satisfy my physical needs and desires. I was totally imperceptive to her needs as a sensitive, feeling human being. Furthermore, I had not been true to myself. I was phony, inauthentic. I had rejected any sense of responsibility to her or to myself. I had refused to make the decision which my espoused belief in Christ demanded of me. I had opted out.

What does this experience tell me about the nature of authenticity—the "way things are"?

If I gained any existential insight from this "lived" moment it relates to the meaning of love. With her I had been seeking love—looking for it as one seeks a treasure, looking for someone to love *me*, to affirm me as a person with value. But I discovered that love is not sought and found. Love is something that *is*—something that's part of one's very essence as a human being. People don't love me because I'm attractive or witty or intelligent, nor because I'm "lovable." People love me because I love—because love is a part of my very being.

Put It in Sound and Lyric

Lived moments can be put into various forms which crystalize and communicate the significance hidden in them.

We constantly need new lyrics and sounds—which straightforwardly report, "This is what is happening. I was the man. This is what I felt. This is the way it is."

And created by the young people themselves—the creators and consumers of culture.

Here are songs written to current tunes by different table groups at two weekend workshops for young people and adult leaders on "Producing Contemporary Celebrations." The first two are from Tulsa, Oklahoma; the others are from San Antonio, Texas.

1.

The worst that I say, you do not hear.
The things that I see, you do not see.
The things that I feel, you do not feel.
Oh, when can we meet, can we join
      Be as one, as one?

At times I long to talk and tell you of me.
But then the words I say, you do not hear.
The feeling that I feel, you do not feel.
I long to be open, but can't.

It seems many times that I can tell you.
What I so much want to say so loud.
The words that I say are not what I feel.
I'll speak when you listen to me.

2.

There is a soul in every man.
Oh, why can they not see?
That life is for the universe
Contained in you and me.

I spent a day without a friend
Tho' we sat together long.
We talked and talked and said a lot
But still I was alone.

He told me that he was afraid.
And I felt his fear with him.
But, God, it didn't mean a thing.
I couldn't share with him.

I saw a star shine in the night.
A star I'll never hold,

And tho' I should be warm with love
This world has made me cold.

There is a face that's hard to see,
A face that's hard to find.
And a voice that I have never heard
Until you spoke in mine.

It was good to hear your voice.
I thought silence was my brother.
We tried to look and show our thoughts.
Thoughts about each other.

3.

Where is the place where we can find ourselves
When we search for much more than we know?

Where is the peace that we know we can find
But cannot tell which way to go?

4.

Hello, Friday, my old friend,
I've come to rest in you again
Because the weekly strain has got me down,
And I can't see what my work has done,
And I'm ready to leave the week behind.
All is fine,
For here is the relief of Friday.

5.

What, O what, does caring mean?
Does it matter?
Does it matter if I care and am alone?
What, O what, does lonely mean?
Lonely means that no one cares.

When will we ever learn?
When will we ever care?

What, O what, does caring mean?
Yes it matters.
Yes it matters if I care, I'll make it show.
No disguises, no pretense, no more
Mask will hide us now.

Now we can really learn.
Now we can really live.

6.

When, when will I be me?
When, O when, can I be?
I can choose any role
But when, O when, can I be me?

Drive, drive, our life is drive.
"Succeeds" is the word to guide our lives.
Drive, drive, drive, our life is drive.
Succeed or life will conquer you.

Mask, mask, we hide in masks.
When can we see we live in masks?
Clowns, clowns, who act out lives,
Who will unmask our phony lives?

7.

From what is he running?
What does he seek
Alone down the highway,
Alone in the dark?

The distance is great,
But existence needs a goal.
Will he ever make it?
Who will help him know?

Running from closed doorways,
Running by himself,
Afraid they won't listen,
Or might not understand.

A high school boy explains "how it is to be a young person."*

Many times
I've been alone in a crowd,
Not knowing where to go, turn, who to see,
Scared of my friends, my family, my girl.

My mother, she doesn't understand.
My old man, well,
I feel sorry for him,
He's got to live with my mother.
I feel sorry for her,
She's got to live with him.
I feel sorry for both of them,
They've got to live with each other.

Me and my girl fight.
I don't know why.
I guess it's 'cause we watch our parents,
Just doin' what comes natural, I guess.

I guess a lot,
But I don't really know.
I don't have any big problems,
Just a lot of little ones making life bad news.

My girl, I call her that, but she really ain't. She's
   got five other guys and they're big.
Anyway, how can a guy fifteen, in high school, no job,
   car, money, have a girl?

Or be in love?
What I really want is someone to talk to,
Someone to be with, to tune into.
A place to go.
But I can't find this, or where, or how.
If I found someone I don't know what I'd do.
But . . . well . . . I guess I sound a little confused.

183

Ways to Start Creating

Here are ways to begin working on coffeehouse (or theater-in-the-round) playlets, contemporary celebrations, original lyrics and music, poetry, conversations' ministry of meanings.

A small group, working through all or some of the suggested lead-ins, could come up with something original which they would present. Much of it should have the aura of the spontaneous—even though it might be scripted.

If it were a coffeehouse play, I would image the presenting group as an "organism of humanity"—an organism of youth culture—working out its one life on earth. Different "types" of its members would be encountering each other in short episodes: (1) trying to find the core of the other, where he stands, whether he is of any use to include in one's circle of people who believe in each other and in something together; (2) crying out of their loneliness for some answering voice; (3) shouting their indignation; (4) treasuring a little glimpse of identity, mirror feedback of some beauty; (5) in anguish and wild joy making their way in a precarious, often indifferent world going to hell, yet filled with marvels of man's ingenuity; (6) trying to figure out the plot of life, what the organizing myth is that can hold their lives together and the world, aware that they are of the world and can't get out of it, but must be part of its history-making. Reaching, who knows what tragedy? plain bafflement? hero journey? turning back; (7) discovering a nucleus of a new beginning of humanity . . . disillusioned that even this is imperfect; (8) looking hard at their destiny generation—what its moment in mankind is about, and how a *human* takes it on.

Each of these eight struggles for existence could be assigned to one person to take the lead in voicing it and developing it, with the others joining in and intercommunicating as they felt moved to contribute how this is with them, bumping roughly into each other, challenging, collaborating in working it through to life.

When the presentation—or the series of presentations—

is finished, we would all have excruciatingly and celebratively taken an interior journey, worked through the range of what it means to be a young person in the world that presently exists. It would not preach an answer—but would open up for each person present access to "possibility that might be my life or death struggle, the expanding and shrinking that I am, the aliveness or numbness I am, my appearing and disappearing."

Here are other ways of getting out before us what life is for us.

I. Lived Moments

A) *What experience have you had that would widen our understanding of life?*

    1. Describe a vivid lived moment you have recently had that—
      stirred you deeply
        shook you up
          made you feel very alive
            realize as never before the *meaning* of something
      when you sensed
        I am able
         I am . . .
           freedom
            guilt
             phony-real
             alone
               thrown into a world I didn't ask for
               love.

    2. Go on to tell what sense you can now make of it.
      On the basis of this experience,
        life means to————.
        The realities I had to deal with were ————.
        to *exist myself as a human being* would mean to————.

Write this out, or talk it out and record on tape, then transcribe and say it simply and directly. Maybe in dialogue form.

If you can, then write a lyric that could be "guitared," or express yourself in free verse.

B) *What experiences are other people having?*

Vivid descriptions of life as it is experienced today, and what sense people are making of it.

What is eating away at people from the inside? What is nourishing and strengthening people?

1. The despairs, angers, frustrations, resentments, aloneness, phoniness, impotence and inadequacy, feeling of lostness, etc.

2. What makes people today alive? Gives them a memory of something they are true to? Enables them to become more human? Not be overcome?

Pick out an experience you know someone has had of one of these, and

a) Describe the experience as it happened, and how it felt as it went along.

b) Then look at it, and see *what it is that makes* such an experience. Describe "not the bark of the tree, but the *energies that made the tree.*"

c) What sense do you make of it? What does it mean?

Now put what you said in (1) or (2) into an art form—free verse, poem, painting, song lyric, dialogue, dramatic vignette, etc.

II. What Is the World You Are In?

Today we are living in a very complex and dynamic world—where something is always going on.

All kinds of people are trying to bring something new off. What any group or nation does affects the life possible for the rest of us. With transistor radios and all other forms of mass-comm, everybody is listening in all the time as things happen.

It's like the whole world was one village, with all kinds of bongo drums beating, sounds of angry and excited people pouring out from every section, all kinds of people dancing their tribal dances of this peculiar time in history that everyone has his won version of. Each tribe is trying to take over and run the whole village.

A) *As you would describe it verbally*

1. Is there something happening in this world that you—
   feel strongly against?
   that seems good to you? Has real possibilities?
2. What, as you see it, is a particular task (opportunity to bring off something better) *your generation* is offered—
   in American civilization?
   in what happens in the world?
3. Is there a sort of youth culture all over the world? And, to some degree, are you now living as a part of it? If so, what are its main features that you want to take part in?

B) *Making a documentary photo*

Go out into the world and bring back a photo or a sequence of photographs which document something that is significantly alive.

1. A photo of *"world in the making"*
   An important documenting of what is struggling to be born in this moment of history-making. Which you feel your life might be relevant to.
2. A photo making visible: a critical instant of a person's becoming . . . a moment when a face (body) lighted up with character . . . a lived moment of a person experiencing LIFE.

187

What is a documentary?
1. It grasps a moment—which we see *into*. In it we see the plot of a drama of life.

   E.G., not just a picture of a deer, or a deer running from a hunter—but of *the vivid nearness of life and death all in one instant.*

   This is one way it differs from a merely "candid camera shot." Also—
2. It is a seeing of *significant* fact—which increases experience, stirs imagination, enables us to be an *"understanding potentiality-for-being."*
3. Vivid actuality . . . startlingly direct . . . presence. "It was a picture of shapes . . . and underlying that the feeling I had about life."

Use as well as you can the "language" of photo
line . . . movement . . .
    lights and darks . . . tones and textures . . .
        Energy patterns in juxtaposition, tensioned with each other, completing and highlighting each other.
        focus and background . . .
            overall design.
You may use color, but need not.
Preferably enlarge the photo to 8 x 10 size.
Attach under it not a title, but a brief quotation (or your own writing) that will enrich people's "dialogue" with what the photo is helping happen in them.

III. Offering a Conviction about How to Live . . . that Comes out of Your Existence

Something you'd very much like to say to "my people" (the people near at hand or over the world) with whom you feel you could make yourself and take part in history-making. Tell them of a style of life they can participate in, "this kind of life the world needs more of," this is a truth that can be expressively lived—said loud and clear.

Try to communicate it to them by writing it out (saying it) in three steps—

- a) Describe a situation where it was operating—preferably an experience you have had.

    So that you could say, "There, that's what I mean."
- b) Define just exactly what it is—in terms of ideas. So that others could really understand *what* it is. And how significant it is. What cluster of words develops its full meaning?
- c) In what spot of world-available-to-you would it be most important to say this? What *deed* there would say it very powerfully?

IV. Who Is Saying Something that Makes Sense to You? What Are They Saying?

A) *Of all the masscomm going on, what do you like?*

Who's saying something worth listening to?

1. Your favorite one or two records.
    a) What do you like about them? (the music and the lyrics)
    b) Their message on the life that is good to live.
2. TV program you most enjoy. Favorite character in it. Fellow running it.
    a) What do you particularly like about the program?
    b) This show's message
        —about the life that is good to live
        —about what we ought to be against.
    c) Some particular problem or situation of life that it presents particularly well.
3. A movie you attended that left some residues in you. In your answer cover the points above.

189

4. A novel, poem, play, painting or sculpture . . . paperback . . . magazine . . . that had something to say, and did so notably.

5. Some particular person that you know personally whose views you began to trust on how life is to be lived. What is the viewpoint?

B) *What do you hear being said in today's communications?* Together play four records quite the hit during your masscomm life. Or go see a movie together.

Analyze each number by these questions—

1. The overall feeling tone. How does it feel to be alive? The basic sound and pulse of life is————.
   According to this number, being a teen-ager in today's world is like————.

2. What words or phrases particularly come through as you listen?

3. How does the main character feel about himself? About people?

4. What style of life is he recommending? The life that is good to live. Mode of being-in-the-world.
   Life means to————.
   What style of life is he against?

5. Is what is being done here *phony* (putting on, playing a game, being something that will sell, leading sheep to the advertiser all het up, commercial and routine)?

   Or *authentic* (the way it really is, really "soul," opening things up so that you can make better sense of your life, saying something *vividly*)?

(7) Sharpen a Few Ideas and a Picture of the Emerging World

Is there at least a fragment of truth that we could believe . . . and with it live uptight to the world?

Yes, I believe there is. And that it can come from "talking and living with" Dietrich Bonhoeffer. If we can get our minds working hard enough on it.

Let's begin with some quotations from his thinking in *Ethics*.

> It is only in the midst of the world that Christ is Christ.
>
> In Christ we are offered the possibility of partaking in the reality of God and in the reality of the world, but not in the one without the other.
>
> The question of good becomes the question of participation in the divine reality which is revealed in Christ.
>
> What matters in the church is not religion, but the form of Christ, and its taking form amidst a band of men.

For indeed it is not written that God became an idea, a
principle, a program, a universally valid proposition or a
law, but that God became man.

And it is not therefore His (Christ's) will that we should in
our time be the adherents, exponents and advocates of a
definite doctrine, but that we should be men, real men
before God.

What can and must be said is not what is good once and
for all, but the way in which Christ takes form among us
here and now.

There is no real worldly existence outside the reality of
Jesus Christ.[1]

How to Exist

These quotes call up fresh thoughts about "Christ as a mode of
being-in-the world." They make sense out of Christ to me. With
them I think I move toward a theology that will stand the tur-
moil, tension, difficulties of a world becoming more than and
different from what it now is.

Christ is God *engaged with* the burgeoning intentions of man
come of age, struggling with man's imperfection, guilts, profanations, ambiguous history-making. He is God *in situation*—not
building a perfect world, but transforming what happens into
new possibility. He is not dead, nor has he left the world to its
own devices.

Christ is a mode of *being-in* the goings on in the world.
(And, therefore, of often being defeated.) Christ is a participating in both God's and man's workings—not as two separate
matters, but as inextricably interfused.

Transforming power is the chief characteristic of the Christ
man.

For too long in European and American Protestantism works

[1] (New York: Macmillan, 1955.)

were divided from faith, and condemned. Man's role was primarily dependency. Man's excessive preoccupation with his own fortunes was intensified. His role was to be baptized and made a church member. Liturgy was to feed him forgiveness. Grace was not something hidden in the folds of life, but was supposed to drip from a sacramental pipeline.

The church has had too little to say religiously to the man engaged in crucial decisions for our common life, to the person fighting the justice battle, to the band of men whose responsibility it is to build a viable economic order and metropolitan cities, to the artist and all other creators. God's chief concern (in the church's eyes) was with man's sin, how he could be convicted of his worthlessness and brought to a cheap-for-him grace dependency. God was not fundamentally with man in "the center of the village" trying to bring off humanness. God was absent from (dead in) the *present* whirl and anguish of the world. (He had once upon a time been present.) Except that for many traditionalists, God had laid down some commandments which man must obey. Christ was safely seated up in heaven at the right hand of God the Father, while his emissaries on earth kept up the flow of worship and words. The second coming was not yet. And when it came it would be a cataclysmic *righting everything all-at-once* apocalypse in which the history-making of man would be no factor, except as a disastrous going in the wrong direction.

But now we are once more concerned with how the form of Christ takes form among us here and now in a "members one of another" group, and how we participate in Christ where he is in the world.

The Transforming Mode of Being-in-the World

Bonhoeffer's phrase "the form of Christ" suggests that Christ is not just the events and teachings of the life of Jesus of Nazareth, to be read in a book, or even the story of the life and ascension of Jesus of Nazareth. Christ is a *mode of being-in-the world* by a

193

personal center. A personal center that is also an intersubjectivity —now "taking form amidst a band of men."

Christ is a verb, not a noun. Or perhaps more accurately, a verb-noun.

Christ is originative personal energy taking into itself what is going on and transmuting it into new possibility. A transforming variable that interposes itself between the present and a mere repetition of what now is.

In stark outline, Paul sets forth the ways in Christ which he taught in every church

> "When reviled, we bless;
> when persecuted, we endure;
> when slandered, we try to conciliate."
> (I Cor 4:12, 13 RSV)

Such is the life of the Christian who participates in Christ. Fundamentally, a Christian is expressive spontaneity—a love and creativeness that, in *each particular situation of life,* feels, takes into itself the joy and agony, the good and evil of that situation, and is not overcome by it, but in conjunction with others transforms it into new possibility which it offers to God and man. We are *alive,* we exist (in the existential sense) only in such moments. This is what *life* is—here and now—every time, every place.

Christ is most elementally love and creativeness, rather than idea or word. The deeps of personal being are form-giving potential. Man is a *becoming "isness"* before thought and feeling have been separated out. *All* the depth which a person is, functions in one knowing, one becoming, one creating of forms in particular situations. Ideas, words, experiences, perceptions, acts, are out of this creativeness-love.

Christ is God's urge to become manifest. To appear. To take on significant form. To incarnate in a son—particularly in difficult situations.

Christ is a specific particularity especially relevant to the *transforming* of a specific situation. And by so doing, makes all things new. Christ is an outbreaking of human dignity in the darkness of injustice, an advent of the love of God and man upon a particular wintered world and impoverished people.

> Think of it, from the iron fastness
> Suddenly to dare to come out naked, in perfection
> of blossom, beyond sword-rust.
>
> . . . .
>
> More fearless than iron all the time
> And so much prouder, so disdainful of reluctances
>
> . . . .
>
> Fearing nothing, life-blissful at the core
> With iron and earth.[2]

We Are to Be Little Christs

The mode of being-in-the world is the same each time and the same for all persons. The details, occasions, "signature" will differ.

The Christ person and process is a *transforming* in some sequence of history-making or of stimulus-response. Christ is an *innovating* intervention, bringing forth something new, rather than a stale repetition and cumulation of boredom, unloveliness, stupidity, brutality, impersonalness, alienation, resentment. The tragic, demonic chain of events, the relentless working out of fate as in a Greek tragedy, no longer have dominion. An intervening vitality has inserted itself. Christ is God furiously—and not omnipotently—engaged in the becoming of this actual world.

This is not just nonviolent resistance (though at their depths they are akin). This is rather a resolute becoming-something-different—and going through a cross event if necessary. For the point of a cross is not that we suffer, but that we sensitively feel the agony and struggle of our fellow man, we willingly enter into a situation we could have avoided if we wanted a safe

---

[2] D. H. Lawrence, "Almond Blossom," *Complete Poems*, II, 304.

and pleasurable life; and instead of being overcome by evil, we exist as this transforming, innovating consciousness and person. Even though we do not succeed in the immediate time and situation.

But we are in the midst of life, not safely withdrawn from the agony and creation, the passion and action of our time and habitat. We are not spectators, but participants; not just intellectuals and clergy, but fellow men. We have not brought perfection out of the situation, but it will nevermore be the same. Some "newing" love and developing energy that was not there before is a presence in the situation.

This is what we should mean when we say, "Christ saves us from our sins." It is not that a man once died on a cross and *paid* to an angry God the necessary suffering for our sins, so that those who claim the gift will be let off. Rather here and now the same mode of redeeming, creating, transforming is occurring. And outside it we are all lost.

This is what we should mean when we talk about being "little Christs" to one another. We are present as a fullness which creates newness, calls out new possibility for our habitat together.

Obviously we are not *Jesus* Christ. But we are to be *a* Christ. And we are a Christ *only when we function in this receiving-transforming* way. "Christ" is not a honorific title we win for ourselves, which we apply to ourselves on any and all occasions no matter what we are doing and are. "Christ" means "transformer."

Some sentimental clergy and novelists (such as Salinger) have tried to picture the downtrodden per se as Christs. It is not without some foundation since there is the biblical "Inasmuch as you have done it unto the least of these, you have done it unto me." To the degree that Christ has taken into himself their travail and suffers along with them, anything done with them is participating in Christ. But the unfortunate person is not a *Christ*, unless he himself is a *transforming* power in the situation.

The antihero of the theater of the absurd and of much

current literature should not be confused with "the Christ figure." To suffer pain because of one's own sins and the sins of one's society is not necessarily the same as being redeeming agent, engaged in atonement.

Why Jesus Christ?

This confusion (and many others) is one reason why we must use the phrase *Jesus* Christ.

Many "prophets" proclaim the inbreaking of the new, the emergence of future in the now. Many voices push many things. So the question must always be raised, "But is this which is proposed the Christ mode of participating with love and creativeness in the becoming of the world?" Not just anything and everything going on in secular city is Christ, nor God's creating.

So always we need an originating occasion to point to, to study, to identify with. We need a *referent*.

Which, to be sure, we will understand somewhat differently and freshly because of the questions and symbolic worlds we have in us. But we need deeds and a history to *exhibit*. We require symbolic deeds, hunks of experience dripping with life, to perceive in *startling* form. We need referent events and presentational image.

But we cannot stop there. We must also be able to grasp *what it was* that was going on in this originative occasion. To grasp the genotype. The DNA. And thus be generative in all situations. What living process is here? What kind of consciousness? What mode of being-in-the world does this person-in-situation document?

Without image and concepts that present the formative genotype to me, I cannot participate in it understandingly. I can only be an awestruck spectator. I am left without any ability to recognize it in other times and places, or to tie together experiences and events in *meaningful continuity* (not just memory). To be "equipped" I must be able to recognize the crucial mode of

197

life in many occurrences. An expression of it, or its hint of being possible, must be *seen* as the same power in many different expressions and productions.

A heightening and freshening of my sensibilities to Christ-in-the-world is needed. And again and again I need to present the *image* to myself, consider it, focus awareness on it. I must be able to feel and vision and think this mode of being-in-the-world here and here and here, now and now and now. Not merely in first-century Palestine. The chance of my becoming Jesus of Nazareth is nil. Nor am I asked to be. But there is momentous choice whether in my here and now I risk being an individuated expression of Christ and atoning.

Christ Taking Form in a Team

Bonhoeffer spoke of the need for Christ to take form not only in the individuated man, but in a *band of men.* We must now consider this latter.

Peculiarly in our time, Christ effectively present in our world is the becoming of an *organism* of persons—a *team* who as a *corporateness* are functioning in the world in the way we have just described. A net that has power to shape surrounding life. A gestalt of relationship, each member participating resolutely and with hilaritas.

> "Bonded and knit together by every constituent joint, the whole frame grows through the due activity of each part." (Eph. 4:16 NEB)

The living Christ is a *net* of persons transformingly participating in the history-making of their organization and community. To paraphrase Chardin, the becoming Christ (the only one we can know, since we cannot know either the Alpha or Omega) is a world net of thoughtful persons, in honest communication with each other, deeply caring about each other, each open to the lure of God to become more than he now is, architecting and constituting world. A body of Christ holding the evil and the good of the world within communal existence.

Which is again to say that "only in the midst of the world is Christ, Christ." Again to say that Christ is a *concrete working*—not an idea or a word. Christ is process spontaneously emerging out of an interpersonal center of decision, fidelity, sensitivity to the presence of the kingdom in each here and now. And so is not limited to church circles. "Everything would be ruined if one were to try to reserve Christ for the church." [3]

Christ is a dancing choric ring of persons in some particular "place where."

---

[3] *Ethics,* p. 71.

(8) Participate in the Passion and Action of Our Times

Blacks and Whites in High School

Here is a partial transcript of a conversation between a young minister and two high school girls. It might be titled "Americana, 1967." Tom is the minister.

> *Tom:* You had some experiences on a bus.
> *Kim:* It was after the football game—it was an away game
> —and a bunch of girls were sitting on the back of
> the bus, and a bunch of Negro boys came back,
> and they sat down. And most of the girls just sat
> there, they didn't know what to think at the time;
> and the boys sat there and said, "Don't get up, just
> sit there," and at the time I think everyone was too
> petrified to do anything else. The teacher on the

bus at the time, I don't think she realized what was going on; if she did I guess she too just didn't say anything. Some of the boys said things, and some of the girls were really scared; but you couldn't do anything, you just sat there like they did. And we got home and that was the end of it. At the time, everybody just didn't know what to do.

Tom: The Negro boys had decided to go and sit there as a threat to the girls, or what?

Kim: Well, I think so, 'cause they just came back there and said, "Just sit there, don't move." And talked back and forth to each other where the girls were just sitting all together, scared to death of them. And I think it was bad that we were scared of them, because they were people that we all knew. . . .

Tom: You mean the boys . . .

Kim: Yes, some of us knew. They were older boys; they weren't out of the school system. I mean they weren't people who just came and got on the bus; they were older, but still in school, and we knew who they were but didn't know them to talk to them. But we had heard that they were the ones who had been very big in what had been going on a week before, and I think we were just scared to death. One girl got up to move, and they pushed her back down and said, "Sit there, don't get up." And we just sat there until we got home, nobody said a word or anything.

Tom: how does it normally work? I mean, if you have so many busses, do the Negroes ride on one and the white students on another, or . . .

Barbie: There aren't that many of them.

Kim: No, we were really suprised to see these people, 'cause they had never been to a game before that any of us could remember.

Barbie: We had some trouble at one of the games—some Negro boys threw rocks at the buses. They broke one of the windows. I don't know what was the purpose in it.

Kim: These were people from our school. The girls who were back there were mainly my friends, and we were all back there just sitting where we usually sit on the bus to come home.

Tom: Did these fellows say anything about what they were trying to accomplish?

Barbie: I think we were scared since there was so much trouble up at another high school. It was televised so much. And we had trouble down in our school— it was started by kids out of the school system. And our principal, he really didn't know how to handle the situation, and kids just tried to get away with as much as they could. Otherwise most of them are really nice, and they are courteous and they don't like to take advantage, but they knew the situation was just right and that this time they could get away with it.

Tom: What kinds of things were happening at the school?

Barbie: I just saw pushing around. The girls didn't get touched hardly at all, but the boys got pushed around and kind of accidentally knocked into.

Tom: Do you have any clues or any guesses what brought it on or what they were trying to achieve?

Kim: I think it was just the publicity of the other schools getting away with it. Now everything is back to normal, and these people are really nice again. Ours started with yelling in the cafeteria, pushing tables over—which was exactly the same way they started at the other school. And I think these boys—the ones who did the tables—had just read that the others got away with it, and everybody got out of school, so they were going to try it.

Tom: So this was just a way to get out of school.

Kim: Well, yeah, and then in a way they thought they could do it; they might as well.

Barbie: At the other high school in our community, just at the peak of the problem, they formed a Human Relations Council. A sociology teacher took charge of it, and the Human Relations Committee was composed of about half and half, colored and white. And they put on skits showing how the colored kids didn't really want to take advantage, but they just wanted to be equal. And they had about five or six skits, you know, really short ones, but they really made their point. Finally in our school our sociology teacher, who wasn't afraid to come right out and say colored and white—the principal only said, "We've got a few problems between different groups of people in the school," he'd never come right out and say what was really happening—but our sociology teacher did, and people would listen to him because he's very highly respected. And after that people were much nicer to each other.

Tom: There is a lot of tension, and Negroes are struggling real hard to know the ways in which they can be themselves, and have the opportunities that other people have. The few Negroes I get to talk with— they don't feel that the system is going to give them even a chance to have a lot of things. Even if they had the money, they couldn't get a good house, couldn't live in a neighborhood and send their children to a school where there wouldn't be prejudice of various kinds. So there is more and more emphasis today on simply going ahead and doing things, just to prove that they can do it. Well, what do *we* do with a situation like this? If you go to high school where there are Negro students, you've got to live with them. There is a lot of daring going on.

Kim: I think the people get along real well. The colored people don't like to try to take over the group; they are in their group, we're in ours. They talk, we talk to them, people in classes. I mean, it's not that we're afraid to talk to them or anything like that. I think they just like to stay where they are, like you leave them alone, they'll leave you alone. But I think they're all real friendly. I know some colored people that I would much rather have as friends than some white people. The prejudice isn't there very much at all. At least not at my school.

Barbie: I think our school does real, real well. I think you have to divide the people not by colored and white, but by the nice people and the not nice people. Because there are pretty dirty rotten colored kids, and there are white kids that are just the same. I would no more want to be friends with that kind of white kid than a colored kid. Some of the colored people are so nice. And I just don't think it's fair, the division you use. We were talking about that in one of our history classes. We had a panel discussion on slavery, and the slavery issue didn't last too long, it came pretty up-to-date right away. And one of them in the library accused one of the teachers who was a monitor of telling a table of colored kids to be quiet, and not white ones. And I raised my hand and said, "I don't think that is true—you can't divide people white and colored, you can only divide them noisy and quiet." I think the wrong kinds of divisions are made. We had a colored cheerleader, Betty, and she was just so nice, and so were her friends. It's not fair to condemn a person for his color. You have to look at him personality-wise.

Tom: Today in many, many areas, not only is the Negro saying, "We are black," but also, "We're not going to pretend like it isn't so; in fact, we're going to affirm blackness, and we're going to say black is good. And we're even going to say, if we need to, that whiteness is bad."

Barbie: Within our school I feel that in a few more generations, and in a few more years, things will be real good. Things are pretty even; anyone can do what he wants to; a lot of them don't want to. Some of colored kids don't want to be in our organizations, but they can be. And I think that within a few years, they will want to be, and I really think that, I really do. Like our basketball team—the starting lineup is four colored kids and one white.

Kim: I know there's one colored girl at our school—she's on the Human Relations Committee at our school—and she said that when people think of white people they think of different groups; when they think of the Negroes they think of one big group. And that's not so. She says, like in the neighborhood where most of the Negroes live here, there are different groups there too. Some of her friends look down very much on the people who were making the riots. I think it's true—when you think of them, you think of all of them together. You don't think of different people or anything like this.

Tom: Both of you have given real good evidence that you are part of a generation which has quite a different vision in some ways than maybe a generation or two ago, in which you found large groups of people who really took it for granted that black and white were separate and furthermore that whites were more than blacks. You said a minute ago that you appreciated your sociology teacher really not being afraid to talk about whites and Negroes.

Barbie: The principal is a different generation, he didn't come out and say colored and white. Now our sociology teacher—he's about twenty-eight—not too far out of school. He didn't even say Negroes and white, he said colored and white (and the colored kids call themselves that, we call them that, they call us white). And he just isn't afraid to say anything, and he's got sociology classes with both Negro and white kids in them and he respects them both. He's a good teacher and isn't afraid to say what should be said. And he did it, and people listened to him. It was really good.

205

Building Youth Culture Electronically

In addition to direct participation in shaping the immediate "village" of youth society in their school, community, church, and action in changing the history-forming in their times, young people in this electronic era must influence masscomm culture. And learn how to use it for their own purposes. For masscomm is the most pervasive force and form of world youth culture.

To do this, they must organize so as to get in on the act.

Here is the shape of a youth radio program first developed in Pittsburgh which later became nationally available. The program is *The Place* where a selected group of four or five young people and a program host listen to some selections from the "top 40" pop records. And in quick comment, discover what the lyrics mean to each of them. Doing "on the wing" what might be called "instant and incognito theologizing."

The convictions calling for such a program are (1) we must relate the skills of meaning manufacture and theologizing to this most important cultural expression—youth's music; (2) current music is the extension of young people who are trying to become human and real in an impersonal and destructive world. A depth of religious questioning, a quest for wholeness and love is revealed in the works of these contemporary music and lyric writers. The songs are not the product of hack writers in back rooms, but authentic revelations of what is being felt and experienced and understood by "the now generation." The writers are conscious of the real questions of life (particularly of alienation and loneliness), and present life's questions and intimations in a way young people can take in.

Such a program is not an attempt to institutionalize and sanction sicknesses present in our society and in youth culture, but to listen to and receive what is being said (not just the "good" records are played). The program is also an escape from being trapped in all music and lyrics indiscriminately, particularly by the inevitable commercialization, posing, and "imitation of soul"

206

that creep into all our cultural expressions sooner or later and to some degree. Nor is it assumed that the number of records sold is necessarily a sign of depth significance or that "we should like it." Nor that life presented on platters is the all of life.

But here in such programs is a most important youth activity. To quote from one of the program guides—

WHY THE PLACE?

Today's contemporary music has become the voice of a generation. In songs and melodies, today's youth expresses his hopes and fears, asks questions, and sometimes finds answers. Through his music, the teen-ager has found his platform; through his music he communicates. The teen-ager is not always aware why he likes a song. If asked, he will probably say that he likes the beat or the melody. But most records put out today have good beats or melodies. What distinguishes the top ten from the top one hundred is usually the lyrics, whether they appeal consciously or subconsciously. Most teen-agers are able to sing along with hit records, even the ones that often are totally incoherent to the adult listener. In that music he finds some form of identity. *The Place* can help the teen-ager become aware of the significance and meaning of life as revealed through his own music.

FORMAT

The thirty-minute format involves an adult host and three or four teens. Five songs from the "top 40" are picked by the teens. These songs are played in the course of the show. Between the records discussion "happens" with the teens. The adult may raise a question such as, "What color do you think of when you hear this song?" The young person does not have to guess what the adult wants for an answer. He may share his feelings by taking the discussion in any

207

direction. The secular and the sacred tend to become inter-related. The kind of conversation developing out of these shows will vary greatly from one to another. However, the consistent excitement and perception of these encounters have led many high school church school classes to use the show off the air or by delayed recordings as the stimulus to discussion.

A GUIDE TO PROBING A SONG

Title: *Skip a Rope*   Henson Cargill

I. The Song
   Henson Cargill is new to the "top 40" charts. The song suggests a country and western background. The style is familiar to the pop audience through the work of Roger Miller.

   The rhythm moves to the skip of children jumping rope. The song writer has utilized the tradition of the street song. There are collections of such songs created by children at play. Much of the trivia in the authentic street song reflects the crisis of society.

   The song writer tries to use a progression which moves from the apparent innocence of the children's play to an awareness that the real evil of the adult world is being revealed.

   Three major concerns are revealed by the children at play:
   A. Parental alienation from each other.
   B. Dishonesty about responsibility.
   C. Alienation between parents and neighbors.

   The song raises the question of whether these areas of parental failure are responsible for the destruction of the young's understanding of personal love, honesty, and love for neighbor. The positive frame of reference concerning family, country, and religion are certainly undermined by this parental example of rejection.

The question of the father eating sour grapes and the children's teeth standing on edge (Ezekiel 18:2) is raised by the song.

The irony of such a situation rests in the fact that the parents in this song would seriously profess the very values to their children which their personal witness negates.

The point of the song may be overly simple. Are only the parents responsible for the young person maturing as an adult? Is there more than the right example that enables the young to be good adults? What about the good parents who are just not involved with the substance of people as they suffer and cry out for need?

This sermonic song and its apparent commercial success indicates an interest on the part of the teen audience to share in the judgment upon parents who have failed them.

What does this song say to its primary audience?

II. Possible probes for dialogue:
   1. What is an interesting example of something you have seen written on a wall or on a button? What does it mean? What is the writer or button-wearer trying to say?
   2. In conversation with your friends, what is the one thing which adults have done to most young people which makes life hard for the young?
   3. As a person, with individual characteristics, how much do you have control over your life, and how much are you simply a product of your early family life?
   4. How should one get a measure to judge the adults in his world? Is the measure or standard different from that to be used on young people?

5. What kinds of things done or said by a child do you think would embarrass a parent?

6. What things have you seen adults say about young people which are embarrassing to the young person?

7. What do adults expect of young people? [1]

[1] Program quoted from presentation by Dennis C. Benson, Director of Youth Ministry, Council of Churches of the Pittsburgh Area. See his book, *The Now Generation* (Richmond: John Knox Press, 1968), for further help in such efforts.

(9) The Inner-personal

**A YOUNG PERSON GOES ON A JOURNEY RATHER THAN
A TRIP**

When I went to the summer inner-city project I was petrified, but in every new experience in which you don't know the people, you can start new and get a fresh image. My friends from at home couldn't figure why I was wasting my summer doing work without being paid. I didn't even dare mention to them the fact that you pay for these experiences.

The first days we were supposed to get acquainted with the people of the community. I had the feeling of being "the rich white" who had felt like I could spend some of my extra time helping the "poor niggers." I mean, I felt like that is how the community saw us.

My first encounter with the community was one of the first nights I went down to the community hangout. I was the only girl from our group that went, but I felt that the six others would never "come out of their shells," which most of them didn't. I was used to doing this at home, but I found out later that no decent girl would think of being out on the streets after ten. The next night I had an offer of $50.00. I soon learned that this community was different from mine.

When we started to work with the people (the object being to work *with* the people, not doing it as a favor) they were friendly and warm—a trait I find hard to discover in people, and one I love. They were generous with their things, and I soon broke off with the project-group cliques and became interested in the community people.

Around the fourth week I began going out with a boy in the community. This was sort of shocking to the parents, but really wasn't that uncommon a thing because the high school these kids attended was integrated.

————Falls Park was isolated from the wealthy white suburb of ————Falls by a county boundary line set up quite obviously to keep "that sort of trash" out of————Falls. One of the kicks my boyfriend and I got was to walk into————Falls and watch the people driving along run off the road staring at us. At times when I took some of the small children whom I tutored into the village they were watched closely and usually cheated with change. I was really shocked and tried to talk to some of the store people, but it was hopeless. Then one time one of my tutees borrowed my laundry bags when I went to the laundromat. He said he wanted to get groceries. When he came back he had a bag of groceries, all unpaid for, and I asked him why. He said, "I do this as part of the family—how else can we eat?"

One night I went to a movie with the fellow I was dating and then called my mother on a phone in————Falls. The theater manager had called the police on us, and we were followed, and finally before we crossed the county line we were stopped and questioned.

The police force of the area was quite brutal and had

hardly any arrests for the Negroes, but would take them in, beat them, and dump them back at———Falls Park. I was shocked that this sort of thing happened to people I knew.

In the project group there was so much to be learned. I felt I was a Midwestern farmer. These people were up on current affairs, well-read, interested in the world situation, all around cultured. I felt a hostility toward these people, most of whom had come from the East. My first real exposure to drugs came here too. About one fourth of the kids smoked pot, and almost everyone except me at least had tried it. It was such an innocent and naïve feeling I had. I do find that there is a great deal more drug use in the East. Quite a common hang-up.

The reaction of my home community played a great part in the effect on me of the summer. I tried to write letters that explained everything, so that maybe I could educate or help my friends to understand my experiences. But what I felt inside—the awakening and great broadening—I just couldn't express.

During the middle of the project I had a real yearn to talk to one of my old friends. So I got all my money together and called this girl who was my best friend at the time. Her parents answered and said she wasn't there. Then they got to thinking that the only reason I would call was if I was in trouble or she was. They then proceeded to read all the letters I had written to her. Some were quite descriptive and talked about my dating a colored boy.

The seven weeks just flew by. When I came home, I was eager to tell everyone of my project. But Mom was the only one who understood.

My closest friend called soon after I came home and said not to call or be seen at her house. Her parents were sure I had had an affair and had called for money for an abortion. They did not want me to corrupt their daughter anymore, now that I was a "nigger lover." I was so shocked that anyone with a good mind, who had been so nice and understanding, could now ban me from the house.

I also visited another friend, and her mother came in and

said, "I really am wondering, do Negroes wash?" I know that it was said in ignorance, but I wondered what in the back of her mind that she must have thought I had seen or done.

I also bought a *Time* magazine and took it over there. My friend said, "Who did you buy it for, your mother?" I explained to her that I had become interested in the affairs of the world, and she asked me, "What does it matter what goes on in Africa or China?"

After visiting my friends, all seemed so changed. I had to leave such a confining place. Mom and I talked of boarding school, and I was really excited. My friends thought it snobby of me to want to leave as soon as I had returned, as if their town wasn't good enough for me. At news of my going off to school, the gossip started spreading that the thing was that I was being sent away to get psychiatric help and/or to have a baby. Even now when I come home people stare at me and check out the size of my stomach and have heard many stories about some of the wild things I was supposed to have done.

When I now look back on this summer, time has made it mellow. The crisis that seemed so close and so important for me (to get out of the community that I felt I was suffocating in) seems gone. Yet I know if I had stayed there any longer my superficial life, and that of my friends —whose only concerns were their clothes, boyfriends, and access to "daddy's bar"—would have fallen back into place, and I'd be in the ol' rut again. I feel I have escaped here to school. There are many of the same problems here, but the people—just by living together—are more expressive and seem to have a concern for the world, other people and their future.

One Inner-personal Region

One of our functions as a friend is to understand another person's *unique* "existence situation" *as of this particular moment.* And therefore gradually come to know the variety of inner-personal conditions which young people are today. The following may help you move in this direction.

In the course of a personal conversation with the adult counselor for the youth group of a church, a high school senior boy made the following remarks:

1. "I can converse with adults, as far as that goes. But as far as them understanding me—it's quite, quite difficult. I know my parents . . . I have that problem with my parents—at least I seem to think so. My parents seem . . . they say they don't understand me. I don't understand them.

2. At times I feel like my parents are reading into my mind, so to speak. I mean, they think I'm doing this for some reason, so to speak, and uh, I feel I'm not. They're telling me what I'm doing, and I just don't feel that way. And I feel they just don't understand what I'm trying to do. My communication is just bad with my parents, as far as that goes.

3. I think the problem is that as a person becomes older, he becomes more conservative in his ideas. I think the youth has much more liberal ideas as many things go, and this causes a conflict between adults and young people. I know that in my family that's the way I feel. My parents are conservative in their beliefs, many of their beliefs, and uh, I'd like to change some things here and there. But, the way it looks, I'll probably become conservative in time myself. That's the way it seems to me. As you become older, you become more conservative.

4. I don't know. I think in some things I am somewhat conservative now. I'm turning more and more . . . being influenced by my parents and other adults. Because I know—oh, about two years ago there were some things

I was very fanatical on, so to speak. And now I don't feel the same way about them. So it changes. I mean I do notice a little change—it isn't much, but I do notice a little change.

(various subjects are here talked about)

5. Of course I don't know much about this. I mean these are just opinions that I've gotten. I believe they'll change if I go into this more, and will learn the error of my ways.

6. I think the . . . something about when you're a youth . . . your opinions . . . you can be swayed very easily by people who can talk—who are very influential on you. Now when you become an adult, I think you have more of a set opinion. It doesn't change as easy as a youth will change his opinion.

7. I think adults are more stable. All throughout the world. I mean, uh, usually most of these problems in the world right now are caused by youth rioting, so to speak. This is a problem in all countries. It's usually by the youth. The college youth.

Our first task is to understand the existence situation of this young man, which is speaking up through his words. The momentum which is *forming* his words. And then ask ourselves what "mode of being-in-the world" is this?

By "existence situation" we mean two things: (1) Is his inner-personal region expanding or shrinking, becoming more numb or enlivened, about to appear or to disappear? Is he more in contact with himself, or more alienated from his own feelings and inner core? (2) What is the meaningful world he organizes at this moment as his dwelling place and arena of encounter? (What is his *life world?*) What is happening to his power to organize a meaning-full world?

Try yourself out on what you would say in conversation with this young man that would help clear and firm his own understanding and help him become in charge of his existence situation. Form a brief response to each one of his statements, so that you would be giving voice to the secret sentences within his words. After you have done yours, read on. The following is one set of possible participations by another person in the development of meaning and identity which the boy is attempting as he talks. The numbers correspond to each of the boy's statements quoted earlier.

1. When you're around adults, you seem to be in a world where nobody understands you. And you don't understand them.

2. They keep reading motives into what you do . . . that aren't really there. And you keep doing the same to them. It's sort of bad.

3. This changing into a conservative—it will be good for you? Or will you feel you've let down your own ideas about things? Where do you come out on that?

4. "I notice I'm not the same person I was two years ago."

5. "I'm doubtful about my present convictions. I expect I'm wrong about them."

6. It's been your experience that you're easily swayed?

7. The trouble with the world is its young people.

Having developed a conversation with him along these lines, we begin to feel that his present mode of *being-in-the world* could be "puzzled uncertainty within fate." Perhaps even "I'm going into nonexistence. Even now I'm not real."

If so, he is like many, many young people.

What culturing should be available? How well could you receive him in his present becoming? And other young persons?

(10) The Momentum and the Tune

Existence Fiesta

At the end of our month together in the class in Christian Existence, we wrote a litany which expressed for us the *new humanity* we felt called to live. It has in it words which a month's study together had made meaningful. And metaphors out of our personal experiences. You may translate them into words that are yours before you use them with your group.

But it is a statement of the new conscience and the unalienated life.

This "existence fiesta" is meant to be read in the "shout shaking the earth" manner that Ainsworth asked the Pilgrims to sing their songs. But also to be sung, sounded, pictured, danced, dramatized, news-reported, made into your history. Put together your existence fiesta.

218

I. *Be! now and here!*

1. Exist yourself! Don't just have information.
   Firmly trained muscles
   Catapault pole-vaulting men
   High over their goals.

2. Become a *human* being!
   spiraling up the mountain.

3. Exist a *life* world
   with a new research project to put into practice.

4. The poetry of the present!
   fish moving up
   the river to spawn in pools
   past rocks and falls
   over the rapids, always working
   swimming violently.

5. Participate in truth . . . and decisively
   drive across the Blue Water Bridge.
   You cannot turn back or stop, yet where you are
   going is not possible to know.

6. Create with others a habitat fit for human beings,
   a meaningful shape out of a fiery furnace of feelings.

II. *Live in meaningful world!*

7. Go for meanings—
   a leap to a higher level, a plunging to a depth,
   a moving forward in history.

8. Meaning is born in the dark,
   bringing out one's being.

9. Perceive . . . perceive . . . experience . . . experience—
   step into a whirlpool to seek the bottom's light.

10. Become skilled at processing lived moments into
    meanings—
    a car on a winding road that travels on.

219

11. And in helping others do so—
    walking side by side with a comrade through a
    perilous country.

12. An *understanding* potentiality for being!
    living out of a tremendous vista.

13. "Speaking words" . . . in place of spoken words—
    the tulip bulb-in-the ground . . . touched by sun-
    shine.

14. Conscience and inner speech—
    a tree of life!

15. Function as time,
    like Lincoln grasping the meaning of the slavery
    issue and stepping to the fore as our country's
    leader.

16. Go for *inter*subjectivity—
    the blooming of a flower which begins to cross-
    pollinate.

III. *Develop!*

17. Dreary more of the same endlessly through life?
    NO. Free me from hang-ups.

18. Mere change? Fashion swerves?
    NO, NO. Jump off a high diving board headfirst
    instead of feetfirst.

19. Develop with new organizers
    leap on a powerful, wild stallion and ride it in the
    direction and the style that you want to go.

20. Continuity and discontinuity—
    a free-swimming tadpole who realizes that some-
    day he must give up his present existence to
    become an adult frog.

21. Epochs of new possibility—
    a stirring of the depths, a trembling to become
    manifest.
22. Darksome Mystery, Abyss of Potential—
    Christ on the cross.
23. Ever-coming God, the Innermost Moving,
    Form me!

R